THE ORIGINS OF A
PARISH

First published in 2008 by Kailpot Press
11 Horsecroft Road
Hemel Hempstead
Hertfordshire
HP1 1PZ

ISBN 978-0-9556860-0-9

Picture credits
© Andrew Rafferty, front and rear cover and pages 7, 11, 13, 14, 16, 18, 19, 20, 32, 35, 41, 42, 43, 44, 45, 49, 50, 51,
© Christopher Rafferty pages 25, 38
© John Buckley reproductions of priest portraits, pages 46, 54, 62
© Mary Rafferty pages 28, 48
© National Portrait Gallery   Portrait of Bishop Henry Robinson. page 26
                                  Portrait of A W N Pugin, page 40
Both images are reproduced by permission of the National Portrait Gallery
Thanks to Father Geoffrey Cunliffe for the picture on page 47
© Fr Stephen Wright OSB and Andrew Dubieniec page 58

Front and back cover shows the detail of the ceiling of Our Lady and St Wilfrid RC Church, Warwick Bridge.

THE ORIGINS OF A

PARISH

The turbulent history that preceded the erection of
the Pugin Church in Warwick Bridge, Cumbria
and the subsequent development of
Our Lady and St Wilfrid's Parish

Kevin Rafferty

KAILPOT PRESS

Acknowledgements

In compiling this work I have had the advantage that for the book *Portrait of a Parish* I had assembled extra material that could be utilised in the present survey. In contrast little material had survived at Warwick Bridge, and that often containing inaccuracies. To remedy this, I have had to rely on the assistance of a number of people, several of whom had given help on previous occasions. Notable among these has been Robin Harcourt Williams, librarian and archivist to the Marquis of Salisbury, who instituted a search of the Cecil Papers for me and produced many letters relating to Recusants and disturbances along the Anglo-Scottish Border written by Bishop Henry Robinson, which had previously seen little attention from researchers. All of these letters deserve close scrutiny, but in the context of the current narrative it has only been possible to discuss a limited section of the evidence available.

David Knight, archivist at Stonyhurst College, also provided me with several pieces of research, which were very much concerned with recusancy in Cumbria. Particularly valuable too was the material dealing with the life and works of Nicholas Roscarrock and an article on Lord William Howard and His Catholic Associations by Howard S Reinmuth. J. A. Hilton's article on The Cumbrian Catholics has been a great help as has been his summary of the Penal Laws against Catholics. Transcriptions from mediaeval documents are always hazardous, and I have been most fortunate in obtaining the assistance of Alexander Murray and Susan Dench. Once again Stephen White of the Lanes Library has used his expertise to procure for me books that were not available in Carlisle. It has also been a bonus that Philip Howard gave me access to his library at Naworth, which contains much relevant material.

Distance, floods and changing circumstances have meant that the evolution of the text has been charted by three typists in Nan Cameron, Catherine Powers and Julie Cowell, while Peter and Andrew Rafferty assisted in editing and collating the texts. Photographs are by Christopher and Andrew Rafferty and John Buckley.

Kevin Rafferty

CONTENTS

FOREWORD

The Parish of Our Lady and St. Wilfrid lies three miles to the East of Carlisle and stretches to the Scotch border in the North, the Northumberland diocese in the East and to Armathwaite in the South. It is the successor to the Catholic worlds of the Howard and Warwick families which reach back to the Reformation. This story tells of the great heroism in Blessed Christopher Robinson and Blessed Philip Howard, the quiet, faithful Catholic men and women as well as the compromisers. Kevin Rafferty has explored carefully much of this history and brings the story of the parish up to the present. Always Benedictine since its establishment, and pastored since 1900 by the Ampleforth community, the parish has had a Catholic primary school, a monastery of Benedictine Nuns at Holme Eden, a chaplaincy at RAF Spadeadam and a Mass centre in Brampton. Today its little Church of Our Lady and St. Wilfrid is in the news as, alone in Cumbria, it is included in "A Glimpse of Heaven", a volume of the most distinguished Catholic Churches of England and Wales. Its construction by A.W. Pugin in 1841 and the retention of most of his original decoration makes it a superb example of Pugin's early style, a style which today is more appreciated through the work of Rosemary Hill. (God's Architect: Pugin and the Building of Romantic Britain). As changes have occurred in the past and surely will in the future, Kevin Rafferty has done the parish a great service by bringing the story up to date.

Fr. Stephen Wright, M.A.,O.S.B

For Mary

THE ORIGINS OF A PARISH

The turbulent history that preceded the erection of
the Pugin Church in Warwick Bridge, Cumbria
and the subsequent development of
Our Lady and St Wilfrid's Parish

Though progress continues to be made in tracing the development of Christianity in Cumbria, much remains unknown. Frequently the information is at best sketchy, even (perhaps inevitably) *ab initio*. The earliest Christian tombstone found in Carlisle raises questions: did Flavius Antigonus Papias, belong to a sizeable 4th century Christian community or was he an isolated believer? At a later date, names of holy wells are not always a guarantee that the person concerned had ever visited the site, most notoriously in the case of St Bridget, often claimed to be an assimilation of the Celtic goddess Birghida. Later still, when dealing with such thorny issues as Reformation history, problems of interpretation are inevitable and not infrequently some convictions have to be revised. At local level, even though it might be assumed that much information would be available, it is often the case that few church records have been preserved, and what is left can often be merely anecdotal. Consequently in providing this account of the survival of some of our Catholic communities I am well aware that there will be gaps that need further research, or even that can never be filled. For two centuries after all, the Catholic Church was an underground institution holding its rites in private houses, whose priests had no fixed abode. Unlike in Anglican parishes, whose records form a rich source for historians and the current craze for genealogy, there would often have been no repository for documents and little incentive to keep them for fear of incrimination. Locally too, however, I consider Aske's Rebellion to be a key event in Reformation history, and have chosen this as the starting point of my account.

Kevin Rafferty

THE REFORMATION IN THE NORTH WEST

Although it has sometimes been claimed that little resistance was made in Carlisle to the Reformation, the reaction of Henry VIII to Aske's rebellion which, was probably more religious than it was political, indicates that the king was not prepared to tolerate any resistance to his reforms.

"Henry to the Duke of Norfolk 1537 – 22nd February

We have received your letter of the 16th. We shall not forget your services and are glad to hear also from sundry of our servants how you advance the truth, declaring the usurpation of the Bishop of Rome, and how discreetly you paint those persons that call themselves religious in the colours of their hypocrisy, and we doubt not but the further you shall wade in the investigation of their behaviours the more you shall detest the great number of them and the less esteem the punishment of those culpable.

We approve of your proceedings in the displaying of our banner, which being now spread, till it is closed again, the close of our laws must give place to martial law and before you close it up again you must cause such dreadful execution upon a good number of the inhabitants, hanging them on trees, quartering them, and setting their heads and quarters in every town, as shall be fearful warning whereby shall ensue the preservation of a great multitude... You shall send up to us the traitors... Towneley, the late chancellor of the Bishop of Carlisle, who has been a great promoter of these rebellions.... Finally, as these troubles have been promoted by the monks and canons of these parts, at your repair to Hexam, Newminster, Leonard Cos (Lanercost)... and such other places as have made resistance....you shall without pity and circumstance, now that our banner is displayed, cause the monks to be tied up without further delay or ceremony.

Letters and Papers Henry VIII in P.R.O."

Norfolk acted promptly, and, according to his account, from Westmoreland, Cumberland and Cockermouth 6000 or so surrendered to him. Out of whom, by the advance of the Council and gentlemen of these parts, 74 were chosen as principal offenders and judged to suffer death by martial law.

Henry VIII meant the proceedings to be gruesome, and gruesome they were. The persons were to be left hanging in the sight of their families and neighbours and not allowed to be taken down. Some women disobeyed the orders and when local clergymen refused to bury the victims these women surreptitiously performed the task. Thomas Cromwell told Norfolk he wanted these evil doers found and punished.

Naworth Castle. Home of the Howard family.

Resistance to the Reformation did not cease there and then, but before the end of the century, Catholics (also called Recusants, those guilty of non-conformity) were very much a proscribed minority, subject to a large number of savage penal laws.

In these circumstances the survival of Catholicism in this country was very much under threat. Some commentators have suggested that the position of Catholics depended, not upon government policy per se, but upon the impact of recusancy laws upon each individual. Isolated persons easily fell victim to the authorities but Catholics who could call upon some important person might well escape the operation of the law altogether.

Against this analysis it has to be said that the continuing loyalty of some recusant families to their faith could not be guaranteed for any length of time and the immunity of such families was always under threat and frequently breached. Families were also split by diverging loyalties and in such cases the recusant members not infrequently were left to their fate. An analysis of the fortunes of some well-known recusants in this area would seem to confirm this assessment. Illuminatingly enough the first recusants I would like to discuss provided a good example of the need to examine carefully the reliability of the documents we inherit. Among the archives at Our Lady and St Wilfrid's, Warwick Bridge, is a leaflet giving a short history of the parish. In it we read:

> "Following the Reformation, Benedictine priests resided when possible with families at Naworth Castle, Corby Castle and Warwick Hall. As some names and dates are uncertain a full list cannot be given here."

The text continues with a list of clergy.

The first name provided is Father Nicholas Roscarrock at Naworth 1606 – 1633. There ends all the information about Father Nicholas, and though it is quite true that sometimes we do well to obtain a complete list of names and dates for an institution over a long period, our understanding of the time when a certain Benedictine was said to be at Naworth is not advanced to any great extent. However, I did know a little about Nicholas Roscarrock and when I followed up these leads I began to understand and appreciate the fascinating career of a remarkable layman. I describe him as a layman for recent research indicates that he was never ordained. Indeed one priest who was imprisoned in the Tower of London at the same time as Roscarrock describes him as one of those laymen who, he was ashamed to say, had shown themselves braver than many priests.

Summing up his remarkable career is no easy matter, since he had such an eventful life and had a wide range of interests. Furthermore, although he is not very well known locally, much valuable research about him is now available. Understandably, a major source is a publication by the Devon and Cornwall Record Society, since he was born in a manor house Roscarrock, in Cornwall in the middle of the sixteenth century. (Nicholas Roscarrock's 'Lives of the Saints Cornwall and Devon'. Editor, Nicholas Orme, published by the Devon and Cornwall Record Society 1992.) The family had lived there since the twelfth century and took their name from the place. His father was a man of some property and was important enough to be chosen as Sheriff of Cornwall in 1550 and 1561. Of the education of Nicholas we know little except that he learnt enough Latin to enable him to get to university. He matriculated in 1564 at the University of Oxford. In 1568 he applied to the authorities to be allowed to read (to lecture in public on) a certain book of logic as if he had graduated. Permission was granted on condition that he took his degree the next year. In the event it seems that Nicholas did not take his degree but decided in 1568 or 69 to go to London to study Law.

Window in the Priest's Hole room in Naworth Castle, Cumbria

In 1572 he was admitted as a student of the Inner Temple (one of the four inns of court). Among the people he met there was William Camden, the greatest antiquary of the period, who was to become a life long friend. Another fellow student was Sir Water Raleigh, who shared his interest in poetry, for both wrote verses by way of recommendation for a satire called *The Steele Glas* compiled by George Gascoigne.

But Nicholas had a variety of interests. Many young men at the Inns of Court spent a good deal of time on subjects other than law. In his case Roscarrock seems to have been pre-occupied studying literature, heraldry and antiquities. Nothing life threatening about that, you might think, but by the late 1570s Nicholas had developed an active commitment to Catholicism, which made him liable to prosecution, for at this time the English government had begun to take action against Catholics who refused to attend protestant church services. In 1577 in Cornwall the house of Francis Tregian, a leading Catholic, was raided. A priest, Cuthbert Mayne, was seized there, tried, and executed at Launceston. At this time too, Nicholas and Trevernor Roscarrock were indicted at Launceston for their refusal to attend church. This evidently did not dampen the ardour of the former. It merely induced him to move to London where there were more opportunities to meet other Catholics and

The Altar in Naworth Castle Chapel

help the Catholic cause by joining an association which gave financial assistance to priests. Then, towards 1580, he crossed the Channel to visit the English Catholic seminary in Douai. There he stayed for ten days before going on to Rome on a pilgrimage. He returned to England about the end of October, but was already under suspicion. From the Calendar of State Papers Domestic we read:

> Vol cxxii April 1580 April 3
> Note of matters to be considered by Mr Secretary. "Kenrick and Wm Whiting to discover Paul Gore the priest and Nicholas Roscaroe."

Predictably, on his return from the continent early in November, Roscarrock's home was raided. Ralph Sherwin, a missionary priest and former fellow of Exeter College, was seized in the act of preaching in the house. Roscarrock was arrested at the same time. On the 9th of November the Privy Council ordered them to be examined, calling Roscarrock:

> "a dangerous Papist, evil affected towards her Majesty and the present state, who hath been detected to have been a practiser with foreign states and a conveyor of letters both abroad and into this realm".

Later, on the 5th of December, both men were removed to the Tower. On the 15th and 16th Sherwin was put on the rack to extract information and Roscarrock was held in a dark corner nearby so that his comrade's screams would put him in the right frame of mind to confess. This stratagem was not successful and on the 14th January 1581 Roscarrock himself was racked. He escaped the fate of Sherwin who was executed in the following December, but he was kept in the Tower as a defiant and harmful Catholic.

Despite his courage and loyalty to his church, until fairly recently Roscarrock has not come to the notice of many Catholics. One of the reasons for that may well be that in the same year that Roscarrock was racked the arrest of Edmund Campion caused great excitement in the capital.

> State Papers Vol.CXLIX
> Names of divers recusants, Jesuits and priests committed. Dr Watson, Dr Yonge, Edmund Campion, Richard Creagh, the Irish Bishoppe Jos Redgrave, Ralph Sherwin, Nicholas Roscarrock and others.

However, while the Encyclopedia Britannica, for example, carries an appreciative section on Edmund Campion, the name of Roscarrock , at least in my edition, is not to be found. Compared with the tension and publicity that accompanied Campion's execution, the fact that Roscarrock was imprisoned in the Tower did not arouse too much public interest, and it was not until March 1586 that an appeal was made for his release. Possibly as a result of this appeal, by September he was released. However, his confinements did not end there for in 1593 an Act of Parliament brought in prison sentences for Catholics who refused to attend church. Consequently, Nicholas endured at least three more periods of imprisonment in the concluding years of the century. Strangely enough his long stay in the Tower produced some lasting benefits, for in 1585 he had been joined there by the Earl of Arundel and Lord William Howard, (a.k.a. Belted Will).

> State Papers
> Vol CLXXXIX 1585 June
> Names of the prisoners in the Tower, and by whom committed. The Earl of Arundel and Lord Wm Howard, Thomas Somerset, Dr Anslowe and others.

Though it seems to be accepted that William Howard's friendship with Nicholas Roscarrock began when both were in the Tower, the generous assistance given by William to the Cornishman was not simply and solely dependent on a desire to

Portrait of William Howard

support someone who had suffered for his beliefs, as he had. Others were helped by being given employment at Naworth or elsewhere. For example the Widmerpooles were recusants and one of their number, a schoolmaster, was executed for helping a priest, and it does not seem to have been a coincidence that Thomas Widmerpoole was given a post as steward at Naworth. However, with Nicholas Roscarrock the relationship was not limited to one of providing financial assistance or employment, for although Nicholas by 1600 had, through fines, lost or sold his lands in Devon and Cornwall, he was not entirely destitute.

In this situation it would seem that Nicholas came to Naworth in 1601 as a companion or gentleman retainer. There he remained until his death. The friendship between the companions was enduring. Both shared deeply held religious beliefs, both had a love of scholarship. Lord William's interests concentrated particularly on archeology and history. He had an extensive library, which included manuscripts and printed books. Other resources were available. Lord William's son-in-law, Sir Robert Cotton, had one of the best historical libraries of the day and made loan of manuscripts and books to Naworth on a number of occasions.

Despite the sufferings endured by Roscarrock in prison, he lived on until he was in his mid eighties. He died in 1633 or 4, but evidently he had been blind since 1621, for at that time Lord William wrote to Cotton to ask him to lend his friend another manuscript saying:

> "though he cannot take a viewe thereof, yett he much longeth to lend his eare to herken to the reading of the same".

Unsurprisingly there is some evidence that Nicholas did not stop working when he became blind. It seems that he kept on producing new work or correcting former scripts, in spite of his blindness, long after 1621.

A man for all seasons, perhaps. But little has come down to us about his life in this area, save from a comment in the household books at Naworth that he once ordered four gallons of sack from Brampton. He may well also be said to have blotted his copybook in local terms with a singular piece of vandalism, in the form of the removal of the head of Bewcastle Cross, which he sent to Camden and which now seems lost forever, (along with other artefacts that Camden collected, such as the leaden cross purported to have come from King Arthur's grave at Glastonbury!).

Chapel and entrance to the Priest Hole, Naworth Castle

Though the career of Nicholas Roscarrock tells us a great deal about the problems facing Catholic laymen in his time and the courageous way in which that scholar faced up to them, a closer look at the life of William Howard should enable us to obtain an overall analysis of the strategies used by a limited number of recusants to cope with the penal laws that restricted them in every walk of life.

As has been noted above, although William Howard as a person of rank was of great assistance to some of his fellow Catholics, he was not totally immune from prosecution. Furthermore, the survival of Catholicism in this area was threatened by forces against which he could offer only a limited resistance. Ranged against him as a Catholic were the Civic authorities, the Established Church and jealous Protestant neighbours who envied both his wealth as a great northern land owner and his influence as the defender of the Borders against thieves and wrongdoers. That might seem a clear enough description of William Howard's problems as a Catholic towards the end of the 16th century, but the story of his life is bewilderingly complex. One could hardly call him a cradle Catholic.

His father, the 4th Duke of Norfolk, was a sincere and zealous Protestant and he evidently meant his son to be brought up in the new religion. In the event, progress in William's development could hardly have been improved when his father was executed in 1572. At that time William was nine years old, an orphan in the care of a brother not yet fifteen. Against all the odds, you might think, William Howard's fortunes eventually were considerably improved.

Roof boss detail in the Howard Chapel

Howard S Reinmuth (1973), in his succinct analysis of the peer's career, notes that:

> Lord William Howard is surely the least known of the fourth Duke of Norfolk's three sons. Although a Catholic, he was not a martyr like his half-brother Philip. Unlike his elder brother Thomas, first Earl of Suffolk, he had no spectacular public career. But because he was not a martyr, he was a more typical Catholic layman than his half-brother; because he lacked high public office and never sought the position of a courtier, but spent his time managing his estates, and participating, though as a Catholic unofficially, in local government, he was more typical of landowners of his period than his brother Thomas. Between the two extremes of martyrdom and hypocrisy were the great majority of English Catholics; between these two extremes we can place Lord William Howard of Naworth Castle, Cumberland.

Detail of a panel painting in the chapel of Naworth Castle

He goes on,

> In a few years' time, the marriage arrangements contemplated by the late Duke were realised: the three Howard sons were married to the three Dacre co-heiresses who had been their stepfather's wards (though one Dacre heiress, Mary, wed to Lord Thomas Howard, soon died). Subsequently, the future Earl of Suffolk removed himself from his brothers, and began a long and difficult (and expensive) attempt to gain Elizabeth's favour. Philip Howard married Ann Dacre. Lord William married Elizabeth Dacre.

Then, early in the 1580's, the two Howards were reconciled to the Catholic Church. They tried to go abroad, but they were arrested. Philip, condemned for treason, died in the tower in 1595 and was secretly buried there. Lord William was soon released, but his troubles did not end there for he spent almost twenty years in association with his wife and her sister in a legal battle for the Dacre inheritance. It was not until 1601 that Ann and Elizabeth Howard were permitted to buy back their estates from the Crown. There was a further improvement in their fortunes when Elizabeth I died in 1603 since she was never on good terms with the House of Howard.

Reinmuth details James 1's dealings with the Howard family.

> Under James I, Lord William's elderly bachelor uncle, Henry Howard (1540-1614), was created Earl of Northampton and Lord Privy Seal; his nephew (Lord William's elder brother) became Earl of Suffolk and Lord Chamberlain. James I received Lords Thomas and William Howard, and professed his love for the whole house of Howard. They were all restored in blood by James's first Parliament.

> But James knew Lord William was a Catholic, and he believed him to be associated with the Jesuits. Although, as a great northern landowner, Lord William was to be entrusted with unofficial responsibility for defence of the borders against thieves and other malefactors, James would grant him neither office nor title of nobility. But he bestowed his patronage in a most useful form: he protected Lord William all his reign from attempts to prosecute him for recusancy. There were such attempts, mostly on the part of zealous northern Protestants who bitterly resented what they considered to be Lord William's overweening, malignant influence in their region. *'The Lord William Howard is a known recusant dwelling in the remote parts of England northward, unto whom the recusants of greatest note do daily resort.'* And they reminded James and his ministers that if only Lord William were convicted of recusancy the King could enjoy two-thirds of his substantial revenues. But in 1616 the most serious effort to secure Lord William's conviction failed. *'The information that Mr Salkeld had*

exhibited against my Lord William Howard for recusancy is by the King's commandment to be withdrawn'

In these circumstances it was not surprising that William Howard tried to conciliate some of his influential neighbours.

For example, Lord William practiced his religion in the privacy of Naworth castle where he had a priest's hiding hole, but he exchanged gifts with his Protestant neighbours, particularly influential ones such as the Bishop of Carlisle.

However, Lord William's activities were not confined to socialising with the right kind of people. For many years he was a stabilising factor in the continuing Border warfare that took place in his lifetime. In at least two letters forwarded to Robert Cecil, Henry Robinson, William Lawson, Joseph Pennington and Edward Gray, as Commissioners of the Border Shires, write with enthusiasm of William Howard's accomplishments in keeping peace in the Borders.

Commissioners of the MiddleShires to the same. (HMC Salisbury Vol 19 p6)

1606-7, Jan.11.— By our letter of the 8th we advertised you of some malefactors of note whom then we had in gaol, as also of some whose apprehension we then expected. Since then the Lord William Howard, riding in person with his servants, has apprehended three infamous offenders, Thomas Armstrong, alias Antons Edwards Tom, John Armstrong alias Jock Stowelugs, whom we certified fugitives in our last list of outlaws, and Christopher Urwen. His lordship took exceeding pains in riding all the night from his own house upon the late Borders to the confines of Yorkshire, whither he pursued them. We commend his great care, the rather because these eminent ill-doers, having long annoyed these parts, could not heretofore be laid hold on.

Signed:HenCarliole
n; Will. Lawson; Joseph Pennington; Edward Gray.

'The Bishop of Carlisle, Will. Lawson, Joseph Penningtonn and Edward Gray to the Earl of Salisbury. (HMC Salisbury Vol 19

1606-7, Jan. 29.— By our letters of the 8th inst. we advertised you of our purpose to hold a gaol delivery on the 27th, which we have done.

John Armstrong alias Stowlugs, Thomas Armstrong alias Edwards Tom, Christopher Urwen alias Gifford Carleton, Robert Grame and William Grame alias Floughtaile, were tried and are executed. The condition of the three first we certified on the 11th, the fourth was a fugitive from Brill and returned from Ireland. The last, having long been a pestilent thief and most infamous murderer, was taken a day before our gaol delivery in the bishopric of Durham, by the great charges of Lord William Howard, whom we still find a great furtherer of justice, and a persecutor of those wicked cankers of our country. So many and so much noted offenders have not at any one time been brought to justice, by whose execution the poor country has received better satisfaction".

This amicable relationship, at both domestic and political level, with the Catholic William Howard, is very much at variance with Bishop Robinson's normal attitude towards recusants in his diocese. As a rule, no special tolerance was expected from officials of the established church towards recusants. They were not merely expected to report on the presence of such people in their diocese but were expected to take action against them. From recent research, evidence that for the most part has been overlooked, gives us a clearer picture of how Bishop Robinson and his predecessor Bishop Mey carried out their duties in this regard. In addition, as with the Howards, so with the Robinsons, we can see how they could be divided by their religious beliefs.

That the Robinson family was divided in its religious adherence can be concluded from specific details that have come down to us.

Booke of Ye Recusantes Certified Out of Divers Counties has the following entry for the Carlisle parish of St. Cuthbert's:

'Christopher Robinson (a scolar) no householder but dwelling for the most part at a place called Woodside nigh Carlisl with his brother Edward. Not known that he hath any lyvinge or maintenance."

Nothing is known of Christopher's boyhood and not too much about his family. The report mentioned above shows that he had a brother named Edward. However, a Muster of the Militia at Brisco 1580-1 mentions a Richard Robinson who may have been a brother since Edward is included in the same list.

The late historian Bishop Foley wrote in his book on Christopher Robinson,

'It is thought that his family were 'temporisers' in matters of religion, that is, while not conforming to the new religious beliefs, in order to avoid prosecution and fines they did not refuse to attend the new services in their parish church. When the martyr's nephew, Christopher, enrolled as a student in the English College, Rome, he stated that his father was a 'schismatic' and that his principal relatives were heretics.'

The future martyr Christopher Robinson entered Douai College in 1590. At that time the College was based in Rheims. (It had been transferred there in 1578 where it remained until 1594).

Since evidently he was already advanced in general studies he was at once entered for theological studies. Because there was an urgent need for priests the College had been given a dispensation to shorten the six year course of preparation. In his case it was dramatically shortened for he was ordained to the priesthood by Cardinal Philip Sega in his private chapel at Rheims in1592.

Christopher Robinson's missionary career was brought to an end on 4th March 1597 as we can see from the pardon given to Leonard Musgrave:

> 'The Queen to all whom it concerns. Greeting. Since Leonard Musgrave, gentleman, recently at Johnby Hall, in the County of Cumberland and Margaret his wife, were convicted of having voluntarily and feloniously received, comforted and maintained Christopher Robinson, a seminary priest at Johnby Hall on 4th March 1597 knowing him to have been born in this land and ordained priest by the authority and pretended jurisdiction of the Holy See contrary to the statute enacted for such offences, be it known to all men, that we, of our special favour, have pardoned, remitted and relaxed the punishment of the aforenamed Leonard Musgrave, late of Johnby Hall, and of all others connected with him in this offence.
>
> Given at Nonesuch 7 August 1599'.

Behind the scenes, both Bishop Mey and Bishop Henry Robinson took an active part in the proceedings leading up to Christopher Robinson's execution. Letters that have survived show their willingness to assist in the suppression of recusants.

John Mey, Bishop of Carlisle to Sir Robert Cecil, 11 July 1597.

> 'Let me entreat you to keep secret the contents of this my letter, fearing if the same were made known it would breed deadly feud unto him in whose behalf I write these letters. This bearer, Thomas Lancaster, is the only man that I have trusted or can trust to discover such Jesuits and seminaries as do lurk within my diocese, to the corruption of many of her Majesty's subjects. He was the only man that gave me sure intelligence when and where I might apprehend, as I did, Christopher Robinson, our late condemned seminary, whose execution hath terrified a great sort

Johnby Hall

of our obstinate recusants; where, nevertheless, there be still harboured three or four more notable seminaries or Jesuits, who pass and repass within my diocese without controlment, such is the careless or partial dealing of some of our justices.

(Holograph. 1¼ pp (53.28)"

When in prison the future martyr was visited by the Provost of Queen's College, Oxford, who was possibly his cousin, since he also came from Woodside.

Dr. Anthony Champney, a contemporary of the martyr says of Henry Robinson that he was of a 'kindly disposition and showed much humanity towards the martyr trying to undermine his constancy not so much by threats and terror but by flattery and promises. But he laboured in vain'.

Bishop Mey was succeeded in office by Bishop Henry Robinson. The kindly disposition and humanity were not outstanding features of a letter written by the latter in 1600 to Secretary Cecil in which he tried to procure a commission to suppress recusants. Nor does constancy seem an issue to him, given his appreciative references to William Cecil, who, when it suited him, "affected to live the life of a pious Catholic, attending Mass, receiving his Easter Communion from the priest,

Henry Robinson, Bishop of Carlisle

begging the Lord legate to dispense him from the Lenten abstinence 'for his stomach's sake'." (Hughes 1954) Was Bishop Robinson unaware of this, or did he consider it irrelevant?

Henry Bishop of Carlisle to Sec. Cecil. When I performed my last duty to your noble father, he advised that I should procure a commission for repressing recusants. God having soon after given him rest from his labours, I would, before coming into these parts, have troubled you for the furtherance of this service, but my Lord of Canterbury thought the time not convenient, until the general commission for the province of York, then to be renewed, was dispatched, because it was thought that would make void all former commissions. Seeing that it is renewed, I have caused a commission for this diocese and wardenry to be sent to you; if you think it of any furtherance to the service, entreat Her Majesty's signature to it. Last December I and Lord Scroope sent you a letter describing the state of the churches of the Diocese. Of those more disorderly, some are superstitiously popish, others impiously licentious; one husband has divers wives living, and one wife divers husbands. They make no reckoning of ecclesiastical censures; if the principals felt the smart of civil justice, they might be humbled, or at least their canker would not be spread so far.

In fairness to Henry Robinson other evidence should be examined that provides us with a clearer understanding of his complex character. In a letter in which he reports on the number of Papists in the area, he goes on to deliver a highly critical account of religion in his diocese in which he does not hesitate to draw attention to the failings of his predecessor to deal with some obvious problems.

Henry, Bishop of Carlisle, to Sec Cecil. I beseech you not to impute my long silence to neglect of duty. I had to know the certainty of all things before I wrote of them. I find here more Popish recusants than I thought, yet the number within my diocese is far less than within the barony of Kendal and deanery of Copland in Cumberland, both belonging to the jurisdiction of Chester. Of those that have been long faulty, eight or nine have within these two months reformed. Of the rest the chief by little and little go out of the country, as the Lady Katherine Ratcliffe, Francis, her son, Anne Denton, wife of Thos. Denton, of Warnell, in Cumberland, Hen. Blinkensop, of Helbeck, in Westmoreland, his mother, wife, and children, Thos. Sandford, of Ascham, in Westmoreland, a non-communicant, and Martha, his wife, a recusant, with all the rest of recusants of their families.

In the more peaceable parts of the diocese, there are some few of very commendable parts, both for knowledge and conscience. Others there are that might do much good if they had half that delight in discharging their function which they have in

Memorial to Christopher Robinson in Our Lady and St Joseph's Church, Carlisle

idleness, in vain pleasures, and worldly cares. The far greater number is utterly unlearned, unable to read English truly and distinctly. One great occasion hereof was the great facility of my predecessor in committing the charge of souls to such as were presented by those who care not how silly the clerk be, so themselves may enjoy the fat of the living.

No doubt it could be pointed out that Henry Robinson was an ambitious man who did not hesitate to appeal to Cecil to get him appointed to the Bishopric of Hereford.

Henry (Robinson), Bishop of Carlisle, to Sir Robert Cecil 1601-2, March 19. HMC Salisbury vol 12 p78

I trust you will pardon my boldness in renewing the request to her Majesty that I may be translated to some other bishopric, when any such should fall void, where I might perform my service with greater safety and cheerfulness than I can in my own country in the midst of spoils and bloodshed. I hear now the Lord Bishop of Hereford is dead. If it should please God, by your means, to place me there, I should daily bend the knees of my heart in prayer and thanksgiving for you. - Doncaster, 19 March, 1601.

Signed, Hen. Carliolen. ½ p. (85. 95.)'

A similar attempt to gain promotion was made by Bishop Robinson in 1607 when the see of London became vacant. Such appeals could be regarded as the actions of a self-centred bishop canvassing for important and possibly well-paid appointments. Against this suggestion we have another letter in which it is made clear that Henry Robinson was carrying out, unpaid, the duties of a Commissioner, for which other Commissioners were receiving liberal allowances.

Be that as it may, it is clear that whatever view we may take of Bishop Robinson's attitudes towards recusants or how effective was the protection given by William Howard to his close associates, individual Catholics took a great risk in letting their religious allegiance be known outside a particular circle. Penal laws against Recusants multiplied in the times of Elizabeth and James I. Because of the importance of priests to Catholics in the practice of their faith, acts against Jesuits, seminary priests and such other like disobedient persons frequently figure in Elizabethan and Jacobean legislation. With or without the protection of the local gentry this area was always a risky district for any recusant priest attempting to carry out his ministry. A good example of this occurred a few years after William Howard's death in 1640. The Catholic priest sent to this area was a certain Henry Morse who had lived and worked in London during an outbreak of the plague and acquired a reputation for reconciling many to the Catholic faith. Eventually he had been tracked down and charged with being a Popish priest. He was found guilty and exiled. He returned to England and was assigned to the Northern district.

A fresh outbreak of plague in Durham and Newcastle resulted in Morse being posted to the district round Carlisle. When answering a sick call he walked into a party of soldiers detached from the Parliamentary forces marching against Carlisle. He was ordered to Durham for examination. On the way there he was confined for a night in the house of a justice of the peace, probably at Alston. However, the wife of this official was a Catholic and helped him to escape. Recaptured, he was eventually sent to London. The fact that Morse returned to England to work as a priest may seem to be an adequate explanation of his eventual execution, but the likelihood of his arrest was not restricted to chance encounters with military forces, for some well known bounty hunters, Captain James Wadsworth, Francis Newton, Thomas Mayo and Robert de Luke between them submitted claims for payment for the apprehension and prosecution of over thirty priests. Henry Morse's name was included in this list.

HOPES OF RELIEF FOR CATHOLICS

From the situation as it existed in 1645, the year of the execution of Henry Morse, few Catholics would have expected any relaxation of the restrictions imposed on them would be granted in the near future, but when a Catholic monarch came to the throne in 1685, a Bishop was appointed by the Pope to take charge of the English mission. This man was Dr. John Leyburn (1615-1702) who was a native of Westmorland, the fourth son of John Leyburn of Cunswick Hall. One of his first duties was to administer Confirmation to his flock, but it was not until 1687 that he was able to undertake this very difficult task since all of the adult Catholic population needed this Sacrament. In his extensive journey he came up to Newcastle, visited several places in Northumberland and then came through Haltwhistle into Cumberland. There were no Catholic chapels available at this time since until two years previously Catholicism had been outlawed, so those wishing to be confirmed met at the house of the local Catholic landlord. By this time Corby Castle, not Naworth was the focal point for Catholics.

For my information about John Leyburn's visit to Corby I am indebted to F.J. Vaughan who provided the following details for my Portrait of a Parish (1993).

'It has been erroneously stated that 426 people were confirmed at Brampton. (The Victoria County History of Cumberland expresses some surprise at this figure). In fact the Brampton referred to in Bishop Leyburn's register is a place in Yorkshire which is 2 miles west of Boroughbridge. The Bishop had been at Dilston Castle, near Corbridge on August 20th and his next ceremony was at Corby Castle, near Wetheral on August 22nd when he confirmed 126 people. A further 23 were confirmed at Greystoke at a date unknown, before a visit to Dodding Green on August 25th. How far the total number of those confirmed relates to the total Catholic population in the area is a matter for speculation'

The following are the names of those confirmed at Corby Castle:

Mrs. Mary Tunstall	Mrs. Anne Howard	Mrs. Mary Skelton
Mr. Thomas Carleton	Mr. William Ridley	Mrs. Ann Chariton
Mr. Ambrose Jones	Mrs. Elizabeth Howard	Mrs. Anne Carleton
Mr. John Skelton	Mr. John Skelton, junior	Mrs. Elizabeth Skelton
Thomas Orlwork	George Shaw	Ann Stanley, jnr
Ann Oward	Edward Hadlos	Ann Stanley, senr
Francis Hill	Thomas Eatsforthe	Ann Robinson
July Herrington	Elizabeth Eatsforthe	Elizabeth Selby
Mary Princkler	Edward Eatsforthe	Mary Duck
Elizabeth Thornbury	John Fisler	Frances Betty

John Farnworth
William Farnworth
Mary Lawson
Ellen Skelton
George Wilson
Robert Bowman
John Greame
Paul Herring
William Morley
Lucy Dawson
Lucy Howard
Ann Warwick
Jane Parker
Margaret Heskett
Margaret Daleton
Lancelot Hodgson
Lucy Hunter
Mary Warwick
John Bell
Amos Hadles
Robert Briggs
Andrew Dodd
Ellen Stanley
James Bowman
Antony Bowman
Mary Lowther
Bridget Whitehead
Ann Farmouth
John Hamilton
Joseph Little

Thomas Morley
Mary Morley
Mary Scharrow
Thomas Stanley
Richard Eaton
George Eaton
George Skelton
Peter Wilson
Jo' Shaw
Alice Whitehead
Elizabeth Whitehead
Dorothy Whitehead
Barbara Crowe
Jane Eaton
Marmaduke Hamilton
Mary Oates
Margaret Hamilton
Ann Bell
Mary Bell
Ann Bell
Margaret Bell
Dorothy Bell
Elis Farnworth
Mary Eaton
Mary Shaw
John Farnworth
Elizabeth Bell
Mary Muncaster
Jane Dickson
Mary Dorson

John Bell
Eli Bell
James Bell
Ellen Bell
Elizabeth Dartmouth
Mary Hudlos
John Hudlos
Bridget Watson
Mary Relton
Dorothy Smithson
Mary Farnworth
George Skelton
Thomas Lomas
Mary Lomas
Ann Farworth
William Gream
Elizabeth Dalton
Mary Bell
Charles Bettey
Thomas Bettey
Thomas Heddrington
Mary Stanley
Francis Hamilton
Thomas Ducke
John Watcheson
Jean Mazon
Elizabeth Grame
Margaret Hatheed
Catherine Hatherton
Mary Hatherton

In the year following the confirmations at Corby, John Leyburn was appointed Vicar Apostolic of the London district and apparently was given instructions to calm down the king's enthusiasm for Catholicism. The failure to act on such advice no doubt hastened the revolution that followed in 1688. John Leyburn was subsequently arrested and put in the Tower. That he was a friend of Descartes, Hobbes and Cartwright, the Anglican bishop of Chester, may have influenced his release after two years. On the whole, the persecution of Catholics does not seem to have abated to any extent. Locally, such Catholic groups as hung on to their religion were kept under observation and the authorities carried on using informers.

Howard Cottage, Warwick Bridge, Cumbria

Since after the death of William Howard, Naworth passed out of Catholic hands, at this time Corby Castle and Warwick Hall were the focal points for local Catholics.

> 'Thomas Fletcher of Hutton in the Forest in Cumberland, deposes 12th September 1716 that he knows Thomas Roydon, a priest who inhabits a tenement called Lewhouse, as part of Wetheral in Cumberland at a £15 rental, held under the Duke of Portland and that about four year agoe, being in company with the said Roydon, he told this deponent that the tenement was his on trust for the support and maintenance of two priests in the northern parts viz himself and one Lodge alias Bate.'

Forfeited Estates Papers, PRO

Thomas Fletcher also deposes at Preston, 11th October 1716:

> 'that he knows George Carter, of Castlesteads, Thomas Wytham of Workington and Thomas Warwick of Warwick all to be Popish Priests of the Benedictine Order, and believes these priests know of lands settled to superstitious uses'.

Forfeited Estate Papers, PRO

Gable end detail

Thomas Fletcher of course, as we now know, was on to something, as we say.

The Benedictine records that have come down to us do give some detailed information of the efforts made locally in the 18th century to preserve Catholicism, but more often than not, it is sketchy.

Among the papers left behind by Father Wulstan Barnett is this memorandum:

'The Warwick family of Warwick Hall, (who, like the Howards of Corby had always preserved the Faith in the district of Warwick Bridge) has furnished the Benedictine with one member of the Order, who, for a term of years served his own family as Chaplain until his election to the Priorship of St. Gregory's at the Chapter in 1729.

In this area there would be a certain amount of satisfaction among some Catholics that they could still practice their faith, but otherwise the clampdown on Catholics continued, well on into 18th century, and even where pockets of resistance hung on, they were kept under constant observation. For example, the List of Returns to the House of Lords were still on the go in 1767. The following sections extracted from the Return of that year give us the figures that relate to this area:

"To the Right Honourable the Earl of Shelburn one of his Majesty's Principal Secretaries of State. In obedience to his Majesty's Commands, the Bishop of Carlisle returns to your Lordship as exact a list as he has been able to obtain from the Parochial Clergy within his Diocese and the Peculiar Jurisdictions therein of the Papists or reputed Papists within the same, distinguishing their Parishes, Sexes, Ages and Occupations and how long they have been resident.

Nov 17th 1767

	Parish	No	Sex and Occupation	Age Years	Years Resident
Cumbd	Brampton	11	UE, a Midwife	55	20
			M, her Daughter, Sempstress	25	
			C, her Son, a Shoemaker	24	
			P, her Son, Do	21	
			BL, a Day Labourer	52	20
			E, his wife	52	
			I, their Son, Labourer	21	
			M, their Daughter, a Servant	15	
			C, their Son	12	
			TB, Husbandman	50	20
			Do's Wife	52	
C	Crosby on Eden	2	E, Wife of A.A. a Farmer	60	6

	Parish	No	Sex and Occupation	Age Years	Years Resident
			M Wife of S.M. a Blacksmith	35	5
C	Cumwhitton		JM, a Farmer	73	) All
			H, his Wife	75	)resident
			W, their Son	45	)most part
			J, their Daughter	35	)of
			IH,theirGrandson	5	)their lives
			N, their Grandaughter	3	)
			EM, Wife of AM, a Poor Woman	72	)
C	Hayton	11	RB, a Farmer	60	20
			RB, his Son	33	1 month
			A, his Wife	21	
			M, Wife of JR	30	5 years
			I, their Daughter	4	
			JB, a Poor Man	70	30
			M, Wife of WM	40	20
			JM, PB, Daughters of Do) W&T, Sons of Do) Oldest about (3)	16	
C	Lanercost	1	MW, Widow Woman	64	64
C	Wetheral	43	PH Esq		
			Mrs AH, his Wife		
			Their 2 Sons and 2 Daughters	Infants	
			Mr. L., a reputed Priest		
			Mr. & Mrs. H/s 5 Men Servts vizt)		
			A Steward, a Butler, a Footman,a Groom and a Gardener; Five Maid Servts vizt. Housekeeper, Lady's Maid, Childrens Maid, & a Laundress	)))	
			Mrs. EH, Singlewoman & her 2Maids	)	
			TA, Widow		
			JH, Widower a Weaver		
			JM's 2 Sons Weavers & a Daughter JM, his Wife, a Son,& 3 Daughters TM Carpenter, Singleman (4)		
			TM's Sister, Singlewoman		
			JS, Widower, Labourer		
			J, Wife of WT a Protestant		
			JH, Singlewoman		
			EM, An Irishman — Labourer		
			Do's Wife		
			EB, Widow		
			Her Son, a Labourer		
			Her Daughter		
			JB, Labourer		
			M, Wife of WC, an Irishman and abroad		

Discouraging though these enquiries must have been regarded by any Catholics who came to hear about them, a few years after these returns were made, a series of events at Warwick led to Catholics having a chapel provided for them there.

From the Parish records we learn that,

> "At this time Francis Warwick Esq., the last male descendant of the family, who had married Jane, daughter of Thomas Howard Esq., of Corby Castle, and had no issue, was advanced in years, and on his death the family property passed to his sister Anne, who was never married, for her life, and on her death it had to pass to her cousin, a Protestant clergyman. Mrs. Jane Warwick continued to reside with Miss Ann Warwick at the Hall until her death in 1774, when she removed to Warwick Cottage and had the priest to reside with her as long as she lived."

The priest was Fr. Ambrose Kaye who built the old chapel and presbytery at Warwick Bridge, which is now known as Howard Cottage.

Coat of Arms on the end of Howard Cottage

Fr. Kaye was succeeded by Fr. Anselm Bolas who served the parish until 1797 and it was in his term of office that events took place in Parliament that were to affect Catholics all over the country, but it is difficult to identify exactly the reasons for the change in policy.

THE ACT OF TOLERATION

By the Annual Mutiny Act soldiers who refused to frequent Church of England worship when ordered to do so were liable to a fine of one shilling and to be put in irons for twelve hours. A start was made when Sir John Burgoyne spoke in Parliament on behalf of Catholic soldiers, even though the appeal was unsuccessful. Some concession was eventually made in 1778 with the First Catholic Relief Act, which cancelled the law that made Catholics liable to accusations by informers. This was but a small concession so it was quite surprising that in a comparatively short time the Second Relief Act or Act of Toleration, came into force. It was a great relief to Catholics though it still left them penalised in so many ways. The concessions may have been made, not so much to benefit Catholics but to counter difficulties faced by the government. It has been pointed out that there were fears of war with France and the possibility of an invasion. In addition, the government was also anxious to recruit more Catholics into the services, particularly from the Highlands of Scotland.

That said, by the Second Relief Act of 1791 Catholics clergy were permitted to exercise ministry. As a result it became lawful for people professing the Catholic religion to erect chapels, which had to be registered, provided they had no steeples and no bells and were not locked during services. Mass could be said in private houses if there were no more than five people. Priests though, were not allowed to wear the habit of their order outside the chapel. Catholics were to be allowed to keep schools and the professions were open to them, but they could not become judges nor enter parliament.

Though this legislation was passed in 1791 in Carlisle it was not until 1798 that they obtained their first chapel after a gap that went back to the Reformation. Several people who were prominent in establishing it had previously attended the chapel at Warwick Bridge. Among them were the Fairbairns who owned the Bush Hotel in English Street. They made available a small building on the West Walls, which was used as a chapel until the establishment of a new church in 1825. The first priests to come to the Border city at this time did not stay long since they found the small congregation could not support them. The third priest, Joseph Marshall, arrived on December 22nd 1800, being as he recorded in a notebook, 33 years 13 days old. Born December 9th 1767. He was to remain at Carlisle until his death in 1854. His first congregation numbered about thirty. When he died, the number of Catholics in Carlisle was estimated to be over 3000. Without doubt his achievements would not have been possible without the generous support of the laity. Mention has been made of the Fairbairns but particularly helpful for him was the financial assistance given to him by such families as the Howards and the Hamiltons, since initially the congregation at the West Walls consisted of poorly paid workers of whom Joseph Marshall noted, 'From the year 1800 to the year 1806, what I received in Carlisle was not worth keeping an account of'.

This situation did not deter this hard working priest. A new church followed in 1825 and in the same year a meeting was held in the Bush Inn, with P.H. Howard as the Chairman. This resulted in the following resolutions being passed:

> "That the moral and religious instruction of the children of the labouring classes of the Community is of the utmost importance to Society.
>
> That the St. Patrick's Institution shall consist of an unlimited number of members, Male and Female, of the Catholic or Protestant persuasion.
>
> That the thanks of this Society are especially due to those Protestant gentlemen who have already given their generous support".

The first post reformation Catholic chapel in Carlisle

There seems to have been one rule for acceptance in the school that the pupil should have attended a place of worship on the Sabbath.

From the Institution's Account Books 1826-1827 we find the names of several well known gentlemen among the contributors such as Mr. Peter Dixon, Mr. Nutter, Dr. Harrington and, Sir James Graham.

The Church of St Mary was built to replace the original chapel in West Walls

Progress for Catholics indeed, and a few years after the St. Patrick's Institution meeting the Bill for Catholic Emancipation was passed. In this matter, Catholics all over the country had no better spokesman than Henry Howard of Corby Castle.

"He started his campaign among Peers and Members of the House of Commons by publishing in 1825, a pamphlet entitled Remarks On the Erroneous Opinions Entertained Respecting the Catholic Religion. He was continually kept informed by peers and Members of Parliament on the progress of 'our cause'. He, being a Catholic could take no official part in any of the debates, but he seems to have directed operations from the wings. Soon, after its passing, he and his two sons were able at last to serve their country, he as High Sheriff of Cumberland and his eldest son Philip Henry, as Member of Parliament for Carlisle which he represented as the Whig candidate for twenty one years. His youngest son served in the diplomatic service.

Opposition to the granting of civic rights to Catholics was clearly expressed in the Border city even from people one might have expected would be moderate in their reaction to the Bill of Emancipation. In contrast to the support given to St Patrick's institution by certain Protestant gentlemen, the Dean and Chapter of the City of Carlisle sent the following protest to the House of Lords:

To ye Right Honourable ye Lords Spiritual and Temporal in Parliament assembled - The humble petition of ye Dean and Chapter and Clergy and Inhabitants of ye City of Carlisle, - We, the Dean and Chapter, ye Clergy and Inhabitants of ye City of Carlisle, beg leave to approach your Right Honourable House with ye expression of most sincere attachment to ye Church Of England as it is now by Law established. We beg leave at ye same time to express our regard for ye civil and religious rights of mankind, and our wish that a complete religious toleration may always be enjoyed by every class of our Dissenting Brethern. Strongly, however, as we are impressed with these sentiments, we cannot but view with anxiety and dread ye renewed and increasing exertions of ye Roman Catholics in England and Ireland. Especially as ye objects, which by their own confession they now aim at, are not toleration but power, not Religious Emancipation but Political Equality, claims which ought never to be conceded, and which would in their necessary consequences undermine ye foundations of every Protestant Establishment. We, therefore, rely, and with confidence on ye firmness of your Right Honourable House, trusting that you will not Consent to remove these boundaries which ye pity and ye wisdom of our forefathers have erected - Boundaries no less necessary now than ever for ye protection and existence of ye Church, and with it of ye State.

Augustus Welby Northmore Pugin

Our Lady and St Wilfrid's RC Church, Warwick Bridge

Meanwhile, back at Warwick Bridge, though the clergy were not faced with the problem of providing a new chapel because of a large increase in the number of parishioners, they did wish to obtain a more appropriate edifice than the one we now know as Howard Cottage. Before anything could be done about a new chapel certain negotiations had to take place. To add to land purchased during the time of Father Bolas, Father B. Ryding made a further purchase in 1802, but the property having fallen into a state of dilapidation, Father Ryan when appointed took the opportunity to obtain the consent of the Provincial to sell the property to Mr. Howard of Corby, holding in reserve for himself and his successors five acres of land. It was upon this land that the present church was built.

Carved above the entrance door

41

Interior of Our Lady and St Wilfrid's Church leading to the Rood Screen

'He erected a good house and an elegant little chapel at the cost of £2.586. Notwithstanding this outlay he contributed by his good management to accomplish the whole and leave the income of the place greater than it was when he first entered upon his arduous undertaking'.

The financial details are rather vague for elsewhere in the local records we are informed that the church was designed by A.W. Pugin and built in 1841 for Henry Howard of Corby Castle.

The erection of the Pugin Church was closely followed by the death of Henry Howard on 1st March 1842. His importance to the Catholics in England has been noted above but it is worth mentioning also that his Memorials of the Howard Family is still a valuable source book for historical students. That he was well respected by non-Catholics can be gauged from the reaction of the civic authorities to his death:

Exterior door hinge detail

The Altar of Our Lady and St Wilfrid's RC Church

'The corporation of Carlisle met in the Town Hall a little after nine o'clock. It was resolved that the Council should attend the funeral of the late Mr. Howard, as a mark of the respect and veneration in which his memory was held by that body'.

'A room in the castle, adjoining the noble library, had been fitted up as a mortuary chapel; and here the body of the deceased, enclosed in a very handsome coffin, was placed. Here, on Monday, the impressive funeral service, according to the ritual of the Catholic Church, was performed with great solemnity. The Rev. William Ryan, of St. Mary's, Warwick Bridge, officiated; and was assisted by the Rev. Joseph Marshall, of Carlisle; the Rev. G. Leo Haydock, of Penryth; the Rev. E. Kelly, of Wigton; and the Rev. Joseph Cullen, of Carlisle.

A little before twelve o'clock the mournful procession left the Castle. The coffin was placed in a hearse drawn by four black horses. The chief mourners were P.H. Howard, Esq., M.P. (eldest son of the deceased), the Hon. Philip Stourton, the Hon. Frederick Petre (son of Lord Petre, and grandson of the deceased — his father being unable to attend in consequence of illness), and Henry Petre, Esq., of Dunkenhaigh, Lancashire.

The sepulchre in the sanctuary

The pall-bearers were William Ponsonby Johnson, Esq., of Walton House; Thomas H. Graham, Esq., of Edmund Castle; John Dixon, Esq., of Knells; Fergus Graham, Esq., of Carlisle; Major Maciean, of Carlisle; Peter Dixon, Esq., of Warwick Bridge; the Rev. William Graham, of Arthuret; and G.G. Mounsey, sq., of Carlisle'.

Following the death of Henry Howard, parish records give us the information that the chapel was decorated internally in 1849 at the cost of £60. After this the archives seem to dry up for many years. We are left with a list of clergy and the dates of their stay at Warwick Bridge and little else.

One of the Stations of the Cross

The Sedilia – seats for the priest, the deacon and sub deacon at high mass

Fr Bruno Dawson
1952 - 55

Fr Laurence Bevenot
1955 - 64

Fr Cyprian Thompson
1964 - 66

Parish Priests
1952 - 1989

Fr Gerald Sitwell
1966 - 69

Fr Francis Vidal
1969 - 89

Fr Sigebert D'Arcy
Assistant Priest 1977 - 83

A START IS MADE AT BRAMPTON

Brampton chapel interior

As has been mentioned earlier, Warwick Bridge did not show a large increase in its parish congregation in the 19th century. This was only to be expected since industrial development in the district was not on a large scale, and the Pugin church was thus big enough to cope with the local Catholic population. Nevertheless, some efforts needed to be made for Catholics who lived at some distance from the Warwick Bridge church who were left out in the cold so to speak. However, it was not until 1897 that Mass could be said at Brampton. (We are told that a special sermon was preached there in 1896). The priest responsible for the provision of a Mass centre was Father Wulstan Barnett. A small account book gives the information that the first collection was made on 27 June 1897. Thereafter Mass seems to have been said on the first Sunday of each month.

Eventually it became possible to have Mass celebrated at Brampton every Sunday and in due time other Mass centres were established, though there is little detailed information about these, indeed most parishioners by this time are not exactly sure where Mass was said in Brampton prior to the opening of the chapel at Craw Hall.

St. Ninian's Chapel is in Ashmore House.   The entrance is the black door on the right.

Father Geoffrey Cunliffe, however, recently recalled his time as a curate in the parish, and supplied a photograph of the interior of the chapel used in Brampton at the time:

> Fr. Tom Sowerby was the diocesan curate before me, he had left before my arrival. I think he was the first diocesan priest at Warwick Bridge.   For some reason Ampleforth Community could not spare someone to act as curate.

> I arrived in September 1949 ... Fr. Richard Ronald Wright OSB met me at Carlisle station in a pre war Morris eight in which he drove me to the presbytery at Warwick Bridge. He told me that the parish was 450 sq. miles in extent and I would have to learn to drive a car. The parish had four Mass centres. Fr. Wright said Mass at Holme Eden Abbey and at the Parish Church of Our Lady and St. Wilfrid. The curate said Mass at Great Corby in the Castle chapel and at Brampton. On Saturday mornings children's catechism classes took place in the chapel at Brampton.

> Eventually Mass was said at Farlam, Cotehill, Laversdale and at Gilsland, Bishop Flynn gave permission for this development provided that thirty or more people could attend. In these locations the Mass was said once a month."

The altar and tabernacle of St Ninian's RC Church, Brampton 2007

Mass centres are one thing, permanent chapels demand much more than the availability of a curate. Nevertheless by 1956 it seems that the decision to go ahead with the proposal for a new church had already been made, for in May of that year a letter from Ampleforth to Fr. Bevenot makes the comment

> 'I feel a shade of reluctance at money going into the chapel at Brampton which is (a) not our property, (b) temporary[1],

There is a more positive view expressed in notes contained in the October 1956 edition of the Catholic Parish Magazine run by Our Lady and St. Joseph's, Carlisle:

> 'At Brampton we look forward to real developments. A new permanent chapel is shortly to be ours - after some builders and joiners have completed the alterations'.

However, the proposals for Brampton at this time had not been finalised, judging by another letter from Ampleforth.

'12th June 1956

Dear Father Laurence,

Your letter is most interesting. It would be a great step forward to have nuns established at Brampton and the house, judging by your script and Fr. Cyprian's drawings, seems in many respects suitable. I shall be sorry if we are unable to obtain it but there are difficulties which (or anyway, those that I see) will not have escaped you.

You do not say (but perhaps your letter to Fr. William did) whether you have already 'caught' your nuns. It will encourage one to buy the house if you have done that'.

Proposals for the house became more ambitious.

'June 1956 The prospects of financial help for the Convent look quite bright; and if nuns can be persuaded to settle there, and under our conditions, all may be well. I shall consult... again on the 10th in view of your promises of help. You did well to write to the Bishop. He may have an aged priest whom we could put there as chaplain, thus removing our difficulty (though possibly creating others)",

Evidently it soon became clear that these plans had been changed. The April 1957 edition of the Catholic Parish Magazine gives a clear description of the new arrangements made for the Catholics of Brampton and visitors.

St. Ninian's Retreat House Brampton (opposite the old Brewery in Craw Hall)

St. Ninian's is a dwelling house cum chapel, with rooms for reading and quiet and a large secluded garden. Ideal for DAYS OF RECOLLECTION for Catholic Guilds, Sodalities, etc.

Here is a sample Day of Recollection' on a weekday.

11.00 a.m.	Holy Mass	11.45 a.m.	Conference
12.45 p.m.	Visit to the Blessed Sacrament	2.30 p.m.	Conference
3.30 p.m.	Rosary and Benediction	4.00 p.m.	Tea and Discussion

The charge per head is 10/- including cuisine. Different arrangements can be made to suit varying circumstances. St. Ninian's is in the parish of Warwick Bridge. Applications should be made to either Dom Laurence Bevenot, the Presbytery, Warwick Bridge or Mrs. J. Silvester, St. Ninian's Craw Hall, Brampton.

The simple interior of St Ninian's Chapel in Brampton 2007

As well as giving details about developments at St. Ninian's, the Carlisle Parish magazine reported a variety of events throughout the 50's and 60's that concerned the Warwick Bridge parish.

Warwick Bridge

Parish Notes— September 1954, Vol.1, No.1

Mass has been said, once again, at Gilsland on the eastern extremity of our parish. An unfortunate day was chosen, August 1st the Sunday before Bank Holiday. Several people who would have attended were away visiting friends; and others had holiday makers to attend to and could not get to the Mass. Only about seven souls were present. Still it is a great thing to have Mass offered at distant spots in this far flung parish. It will help to keep the Faith alive, and no doubt seeds of grace are sown in this way.

We have a few Catholics living in the Ainstable district, about ten miles from the church. There is no transport for them on Sundays, and they have not been able to attend Mass except on the rarest occasions. We are glad to say we are now able to do something for them. On the 4th Sunday of the month there is an Evening Mass at Brampton at 6.30 p.m., and we are able to send our parish bus to pick them up and bring them along. This should prove to be of great benefit to them. Possibly we may be able to do the same for them on Holidays of Obligation when there is an Evening Mass both in the Church and at Brampton at 7.30 p.m. But all this transport business is very expensive, and our funds are low. We urge our parishioners to be active in gathering in financial support.

Colonel Elwes

It is with the deepest regret that we chronicle the death of Colonel Geoffrey Elwes at Warwick Hall in the evening of April 24th.   Since these are local notes, we leave it to others to talk of his saintly father, of the Dream of Gerontius, of his own part in the affairs of Lincolnshire and Northampton. We are concerned only with the simple things, such as his love of trees, of his delight in improving the grounds of his lovely home, of his Cumbrian activities as a magistrate and as High Sheriff of the county in 1950. He figured in an unique ceremony when he was welcomed to Mass by Doctor Gerald Sheehan, the only Catholic ever to have been Mayor of Carlisle since the Reformation.

August 1957

The holiday season is notable for the number of friends who come gathering themselves into our midst and whom we surely welcome with open arms.   Besides Fr. Christopher Lamb and Fr. Maurice Bevénot, SJ, there are students from the Beda College in Rome, and a press of Boy Scouts from Stonyhurst who come eagerly to revisit this smiling Vale of Eden in the parish of Our Lady and St. Wilfred's.

December1957 - The Fortnightly Club

We have to thank Col. Levin of Corby for the new notice-board design to adorn the entrance to St. Ninian's from the road. The frame is teak, to match the timber of the crucifix nearby. The printed notice is shielded behind a sheet of Perspex, very tough; the lettering is Perpetua. A handsome piece of work.

Spadeadam - The Rocket Site

Until two years ago Spadeadam was one of the least inhabited areas of England, given over to the Forestry Commission, who were planting acre upon acre with conifers. Then, Whitehall chose the boggy moors for an experimental rocket site where, remote from civilisation, the scientists could test rockets and their engines for the ever-complicating business of modern war.

Roads had to be built in the empty spaces, where cranes and curlews had hitherto held undisputed sway. Armies of men were recruited for the Herculean task and a camp was built, a few miles north of Gilsland. Many of the workers who came were Irish, and it was decided that for everybody's good a priest ought to live among them. A priest was seconded from the diocese of Dublin, Father Daniel O'Scannell, and a year ago he came to take up his desolate dwelling in the wastes.

September 1960 - Fr. Bevenot

Dr. Laurence Bevenot, O.S.B., was taken ill suddenly in August and had to enter the Cumberland Infirmary for a time. This came as a real blow as Fr. Thompson, O.S.B., was away on holiday. However, Fr. Maurice Bevenot, S.J., who was staying with his brother, has been looking after the parish of Warwick Bridge, assisted by Fr. Francis Vidal, O.S.B., until relieved by Fr. Owen McSwiney, O.S.B., who in turn was relieved by Fr. Kieran Corcoran, O.S.B.

The latest reports on Fr. Laurence are that he is making excellent progress and we look forward to his early return to the parish in good health. Meanwhile he has our prayers.

Warwick Bridge - April 1966, No.4

It was about a year ago that we commented in these notes that the ground was just being broken for the erection of some forty new Council houses in a field on the other side of the Broadwath road from the church. Work has been carried out quickly and efficiently by the firm of Laing, with the result that some of the houses are already being lived in…Now on the other side of the main road, on the way to little Corby, a fresh group of houses, the result of private enterprise, is beginning to spring up, and rumour has it that some forty acres or more will be covered; so the little group of hamlets, Warwick bridge, Little Corby, and Corby Hill, will be welded into a compact mass.

It is impossible not to speculate on what the effect of all this may be in a few years on our local congregation. Pugin's little church is already nearly filled to capacity at one Mass on Sundays, but the provision of a second Mass in a parish where two priests already have six Sunday Masses between them would raise far-reaching problems.

We are still faced with the necessity of trying to obtain aided-status for our school, which now has more than forty children. Meanwhile costs are heavy, and the success of the annual Fete, to be held this year on June 4th at Corby Castle through the kindness of Mr. and Mrs. Lawson, is a matter of real importance to us".

CHANGES IN THE CHURCH AND IN THE PARISH

At the end of the sixties, judging by the entry in the Carlisle Herald about new houses being built in the Warwick Bridge area that would bring extra Catholics into the parish, there would seem to have been a degree of optimism about the future of Our Lady and St Wilfrid's. In practice, from that point up to and including the present situation, the parish has undergone a process of withdrawal from many of its activities. Out has gone the chapel at Corby, the chapel at Warwick Hall, Holme Eden Abbey and the school. In some respects we seem to have gone back to a situation which is less satisfying than that which existed in the fifties. About that time, as Fr Geoffrey Cunliffe wrote, 'Mass was said at Farlam, Cotehill, Laversdale and Gilsland. Bishop Flynn gave permission for this development provided that thirty or more people could attend'.

Fr Edmund Hatton 1989–99

The parish of course has also been affected by changes in the Church as a whole, the replacement of Latin in the liturgy by the mother tongue, the priest facing the congregation when saying Mass, the greater involvement of the laity in the running of the parish and the ecumenical movement. All this, plus the beneficial effects that it was hoped would accrue from the impact of Vatican Two, might well have been expected to produce a thriving and vibrant parish. In practice, it does not appear that the development of the activities of the parish has lived up to expectations. On the positive side, in 1991 the parish celebrated the 150 years of the Pugin Church at Warwick Bridge.

Fr. Hatton wrote of it thus:

> "1991 has been an important year for the small parish of Warwick Bridge. In May, as you reported, we had a visit from Cardinal Hume to celebrate the 150th Anniversary of this Pugin Church for worship. We had a summer of celebrations and we ended up with a visit from the Abbot of Ampleforth on Sunday the 1st December 1991 to bless a new altar for the Church.
>
> The Bishop visited the parish in the early summer and gave his approval to the proposal to have an altar facing the people and at the same time suggested that the relics of St. Petronia which the parish is privileged to possess might be placed under

this altar because "this would put you right in the tradition of the catacombs." This initiated two courses of action; firstly the relics; the parish has two reliquaries, one is large and of Baroque type, the other is a very heavy brass Gothic type reliquary. Both contained decorated boxes. If the relics were to be put under the altar it seemed sense to put all the relics into one box and into one reliquary. Due permissions having been obtained, Monsignor Gregory Turner VG came to the parish and opened one box in the presence of a parishioner Dr. Stitt. Inside that box we found a large part of the skeleton of St.Petronia which Dr. Stitt said was of a girl aged about 10 years. There was also a broken Roman phial which had contained her blood and which someone in the past had wrapped in parchment. Dr. Stitt was able to identify all the bones except three and they were reverently replaced in the box and tied up once again with ribbon and resealed. The other box was found to contain her name which came from the stone placed over the loculus in the Priscilla Catacomb in Rome. Because this was a large bit of stone we have not been able to put all the relics in one box but the brass Gothic reliquary now lies under the altar with her remains".

The 150th anniversary of the Pugin church was followed in 1995 by celebrations for St Ninian's, Brampton, centenary. All very satisfying but, as mentioned earlier, the parish has problems to face not clearly envisaged at the beginning of the nineties.

In this situation I considered it appropriate to try to obtain a clearer picture of how such problems have affected the congregations of Our Lady and St Wilfrid and St Ninian's. Consequently several parishioners were invited to put into writing what the parish meant to them. A summary of their views is given below.

Dorothy Dubieniec

It was in 1990, some eighteen months after my husband's death that I moved to Scotby, from Sheffield, to be near my youngest son, Stephen, and his family, at Low Cotehill.

Shortly after I arrived, I asked about the nearest Catholic Church, and was directed to Warwick Bridge. The following Sunday, I set out for Our Lady and St. Wilfrid's Church, missed the entrance, drove past, turned at the traffic lights, came down Corby Hill, and there it was!

The warmth of welcome, the friendliness of those that I met, and the beauty of this small church gave me a sense of belonging; over the years this has increased and it has become a large part of my life.

Father Edmund came to the Parish some months before I arrived, and I watched the congregation grow, and with it, the increase of activities within the parish.

The opening of the Parish Room in the Stables, gave a meeting place, and many happy events and evenings which we shared with our Brampton friends. I think we were all, in turn, volunteered by Father Edmund, to do some small task or other, and who could say 'No!'

In 1995 I moved to Warwick Bridge, anticipating the day when I would no longer be able to drive, and not able to get to the church.

Over the years there have been many changes, some inevitable, some unnecessary, but I am so glad that I came here.

Pauline Chatterjee

I have been in the Parish for nearly 30 years. There have been many changes in that time.

The biggest change affecting any church today is the shortage of priests. We lost our full time parish priest in 2001. It was a big blow to all of us causing a great feeling of uncertainty in the Parish. We now have Fr. Stephen Wright from Friday afternoon until Monday Morning. Saturday evening Mass and 2 Masses on Sunday morning, one in Brampton and one at Warwick Bridge are well enough attended - indeed during the Summer months at Brampton it can be standing room only.

A fairly recent development is the children's ministry run by parents - this makes coming to Mass more interesting for the children and less wearing for the parents - just a pity the parents have to miss the liturgy of the word.

Nowadays all decisions like the above come from the Pastoral Council. Decisions are therefore made by the parishioners through their elected representatives. It is good to see younger people being elected to the Council.

A permanent member of the Council is our deacon. Having married (or unmarried) deacons in the Church is a welcome and necessary change, going someway to offset the shortage of priests. The work, though, is hard when the Deacon is also holding down a full time job. We need to train another Deacon but this takes money and 3 years training so our problem is not going to be solved immediately.

We have parishioners involved in other ministries, i.e. music, readers, welcomers, cleaners, flower arrangers etc. Quite important amongst these ministries is the Eucharistic Minister. We have several but not enough. As well as helping at Mass, they take Holy Communion to the sick and take Eucharistic services as necessary. Recently we had to reduce the Eucharistic service at Brampton from every week to alternate weeks because of the shortage. It is so important that our sick and housebound can receive the Blessed Sacrament regularly.

Tony Farrell

In my life I have seen many changes within the Church from the Latin mass of my early years to today's modem liturgy. Like most people I do not necessarily enjoy changes but bearing in mind my wish to be 'a docile member of the Church' I have always accepted them. However, I do lament the seeming decline in definitive leadership and guidance of the Church of my youth; it is the discipline and leadership of the Church that has often attracted converts and is frequently cited as a reason to join the Church. We are still perceived as a disciplined religion, but for members within the Church, much has been diluted and faded with changes. I have in mind such disciplines as the Friday abstinence from meat and a meaningful fast before receiving Holy Communion. Even attendance at Sunday mass now seems to be on a basis of 'if you can fit it in' among some members.

In our own Parish I believe we have a thriving Church and although most fortunate to have the Parish based on a gem of a Pugin Church at Warwick Bridge, we could really do with a much larger Church, probably in Brampton. I know this would be a problem as nobody would consider making the Pugin Church redundant. In many ways this problem goes hand in hand with the fact that we have no resident Parish Priest, but if the Parish had not been part of Ampleforth Abbey I wonder if it would have been possible for the Parish to have recruited a priest from abroad.

A matter of current concern is the high rate of young people lapsing from the Church. Of course our Parish is a microcosm of the Church and the problem is widespread especially in the Western world. There have recently been some worrying predictions in the press about Church attendance among UK Christian Churches. Where have we gone wrong? For myself I lay much of the blame on our media. The press, magazines and television know few bounds and do not hesitate to plumb new depths, but at the end of the day it is our fault because we accept it. However, we are fortunate to have an excellent Catholic press and I find the Catholic papers a great source of Church news, instruction, informed Catholic opinion, and inspiration. I suspect that they are not widely read by members of the Church and I would like to see more encouragement given to supporting it from the pulpit and bulletins. A Catholic press is important and if we are to have one we must support it.

Our future hope must lie in our Catholic schools and teachers. They are so important and although we have no parish school, Carlisle is well served by Catholic schools, which we must support.

The Pastoral Council 2008 Simon Strickland, Anthony Farrell, Martin Simpson (Chair), John Buckley, Deacon Bill Kirkley, Fr. Stephen, Tim Davies (secretary), Helen Mackay

H Lawson Pastoral Council Chairman.

Change is often alarming and in relation to our parish it has its good side as well as the less welcome. The days when we had a permanent Parish Priest, and I remember when we had two, were "comfortable" in that we knew that all was being looked after. From the sick and the bereaved to the services and ritual, from the accounting to the care of property, all was taken care of.

The new lay-led parish impinges on all of us in an unexpected way. Suddenly everything needs to be done — things that we did not even know were being done — and we are the only ones to do them. All the very many activities of the parish become very evident and it is not always easy to find a willing suitable person to do them. Personality clashes can arise when teamwork is looked for. Thankfully we have a Deacon without whom we would be at a great disadvantage. At Warwick Bridge we are so fortunate in still being supplied by the Abbey to cover weekend Masses and so some of what I said earlier still applies. However, we are all awakened from our "comfortable status" to put our shoulders to the wheel.

The modern lay-led status has to some extent produced a more active parish community; it must, otherwise the parish will wither. It is noticeable and worrying that, like the advancing average age of the Clergy, the average age of our parish helpers is also quite high. There are not many youthful parishioners that are not away most of the year. We must therefore all continue to "plough our furrow."

All in all as a parish we must not look back, but forward - less easy the older you get. One of our greatest challenges must be to encourage the youth to carry on our invaluable tradition.

The Parish as seen by a Deacon and his family

It was very hard to say 'No' to Fr Edmund Hatton when he would ask people, in his disarming manner, to take on various tasks. Most of the time he would intercept parishioners as they were leaving church after mass, but on this occasion he rang Bill Kirkley and asked if he could, unusually, call to see him — "within the hour". Fr Edmund told Bill that the parish wanted a deacon and it had suggested him. The parishioners had been praying about, and contemplating this big step for some weeks, and had been asked to fill in a short questionnaire, giving their views on the matter. For their part. Bill, his wife Valerie and son Aidan were not convinced that a deacon was necessary in any case, so they were ill prepared for this news. Bill's reaction was that he did not consider himself suitable for the role. He gave his initial reactions but Fr Edmund asked him to carefully consider the request. Over the ensuing weeks it gradually became increasingly obvious to Bill that he would eventually agree to accept a place on the Diaconate Training Programme run by the Diocese of Lancaster.

Before being accepted onto the Training Programme. Bill had to attend an interview at Lancaster before a panel comprising the bishop and several priests. Valerie was invited to attend a meeting with a sister who was part of the training team. Following this she joined Bill towards the end of his interview so that the panel could meet her. Having successfully cleared this final hurdle, Bill and Valerie were invited to meet the other successful candidates for that year's intake, and their wives. The three-year training programme involved sessions at Lancaster covering a raft of subjects designed to prepare the candidates for the ministry. Following the completion of training, to the satisfaction of both the student and the Director of Diaconate Training, Bishop John Brewer performed the first ordination in the life of the Church of Our Lady and St Wilfrid. Everyone involved in their formation was aware that deacons have many commitments, being in the main, family men. It was stressed during the discernment process that when there are conflicting calls on a deacon's time that the first priority is his family followed by work, and only then, his diaconal duties.

In practice, fitting the role of deacon into Bill's already busy life was very much a balancing act. As well as working full time in Her Majesty's Customs and Excise there was also the family farm and guesthouse business to fit in. The deacon's threefold ministry of Charity, Word and Altar meant that Bill endeavoured to be available for those who needed his help, to preach at regular intervals, and to take part in as many parish liturgies as possible. As well as this he was an ex-officio member of the Pastoral Council and Finance Committee. Some sort of balance had been gradually achieved by the time that the Abbot of Ampleforth announced that Fr Cassian Dickie, the then parish priest, was to be whisked away to Knaresborough. There would be no longer a full time resident priest and a member of the Bamber Bridge team would officiate at weekends only. Just as Fr Cassian drove out of the car park at Warwick Bridge for the last time as parish priest, the telephone rang in the parish office and a local undertaker announced the death of a parishioner. From that moment Bill realised that the workload had dramatically increased. He also for the first time, appreciated just how much work and responsibility the various incumbents of the presbytery had shouldered over the years and the debt of gratitude that was due to them. Then began the task of distributing the administrative load more widely between the visiting priest, the parish secretary and the chairmen of the Pastoral Council and Finance Committee, so demonstrating that in the medium term the parish mission would continue. Having established a degree of stability over a period of time, thoughts turned to contemplating what the future would bring for the parish.

Helen Jackson

The most predominant memory that I have about the first Mass I attended at St Ninian's was of how welcoming everybody was; from the warm greeting from Father Edmund, who seemed genuinely pleased that I had moved into the parish, to the "welcomers" urging me to have a coffee after Mass. This feeling of inclusion continued, and was particularly appreciated after my children were born. It ranged from baptismal messages from the Legion of Mary, to supportive comments when baby was crying or toddler throwing a tantrum during Mass. I think one of the strengths of our parish is the warmth of the social support, which the community provides.

When I moved to the parish there were perhaps just two people in the congregation who looked younger than me. Over the past ten years more young families are attending Mass. I was lucky enough to have been brought up in a city and attended a Catholic school. With no Catholic school within the parish I feel there is a need to provide our youngsters with liturgy at their level. Children hear God's Word with greater meaning when its proclamation and explanation are designed especially for them. I know that the adults/parents who lead children in the Liturgy of the Word find greater richness and new life in God's Word as they read and ponder the Scriptures in preparation for sharing them with the parish children. In this respect, everyone involved benefits. Father Stephen has been so supportive of the young people and the introduction of services for children at certain times of the year such as Easter and Christmas, has helped to sustain their interest and involvement in the Parish. I do believe we need to think about the future. Many of the children will be teenagers in a few years time. How do we retain the youth of our parish? I think the key to this is involvement. The more involved someone is, the more they feel part of that community and valued for their contribution.

I feel there is a good balance between "modern" and "traditional" practices. I know the young ones enjoy dancing with shakers to lively recessional hymns, but they will also have fond and lasting memories of events such as Corpus Christi and May processions and the crowning Our Lady. They benefit from the support, encouragement and guidance of older parishioners, and their fellowship with both young and old at Sunday Mass. It is often easy to let trivial matters inflate and obscure the true meaning of why we meet together; to celebrate the Eucharist. Let us celebrate what we do have in our parish; a warm, welcoming inclusive Catholic community, open to growing through Christ's love, nurtured and fed by the Sacraments.

The Voices of some Young Parishioners

Every Sunday since I was born I would go to mass at St. Ninian's. After my first Holy Communion, St. Ninian's became an even more important part of my life. I have made a lot of good friends through church. I think St. Ninian's is special because we have lots of 'get-togethers' like barbeques and ceilidhs, to raise money for the church, but mainly to bring people together. Every service at church is different and really interesting. I really enjoy going to church. It's such a great atmosphere and is a great place to be.

The people I meet at Church do seem to be kinder and nicer than most people. I don't really talk about it to my friends at school. They're not Catholics, although we have lots of family and other friends who are.

Although St. Ninian's and Our Lady's are supposed to be one parish, I think that St. Ninian's has a much more homely, down to earth feel about it because there are more people of my own age and young families.

Just because we go to church, I don't think that we're better than other people. Many people are atheists and don't believe in God at all, but still do good things. The Church should be open to all people - it worries me that there might be people that feel unwelcome, perhaps because they talk the wrong way or don't have the right background. I wouldn't want to join a group that treated me like that. Also, if people have done bad things in the past, then they shouldn't be kept out.

Just pray and ask for guidance. I find it helps me when I am worried or have a problem.

I am glad I am a Catholic. I find the instruction and advice helpful. I don't always feel like going to Mass, but I go willingly and am usually glad I have made the effort.

I leave it to the reader to make any assessment of the opinions expressed above by some of the parishioners.

THE VIEW FROM THE PULPIT

In times of crisis one sometimes hears the comment that nothing can be done to remedy the situation. With this in mind, I asked the last resident parish priest of Our Lady and St Wilfrid to give a summary of his experience during his stay at the parish.

Fr Cassian Dickie

"Warwick Bridge was not my first parish, but it was the first in which I was to spend a reasonable period of time. The Second Vatican Council is in effect an ongoing process, and one has had to contend with a diversity of views among parishioners. There are I think signs that the most extreme views are in retreat. It does in fact seem to be the case that many of our younger priests might be described as ultra orthodox.

Music has presented great problems since groups of parishioners exist whose views are simply not compatible. Does the priest sacrifice community unity and provide separate liturgies, in almost any parish this seems to be a no win situation.

Whilst at Warwick Bridge I always felt that the priest had to function in a community wider than the Catholic parish. I thus found myself in the Carlisle Rotary Club. It seems to me to be important that others see the catholic priest as a human being. Involvement outside our own immediate circle can often highlight for us problems in our midst, which have simply passed us by. We have much to learn from other parishes and I sometimes felt at Warwick Bridge that I was trying to reinvent the wheel. Being too parochial is not an advantage. We need to be aware of the whole Catholic Church not just our own patch.

There are new needs and problems, which need to be tackled. We would foolish to think that the world of drugs taking and the other social problems of today do not reach places like Warwick Bridge. I was very impressed by the young people I met at Warwick Bridge, but it is very difficult to be young and facing the problems of today's world. Unless we expend a considerable effort on the young our future will be bleak indeed.

One of the great benefits at 'Warwick 'Bridge was the excellent relationship between local clergy. I was made to feel very much at home. I owe a debt of gratitude to Mgr Greg Turner for his support. And indeed I still feel a strong bond with Cumbria and all things Cumbrian. It is still where I spend my spare time and come every week to meet with the young men at The Cenacolo Community who are trying to prepare themselves for their return to the world after resolving problems in their lives.

For a small parish in terms of parishioners Warwick Bridge was blessed with two permanent deacons and I am very grateful for the assistance provided by Gib and Bill. In my present diocese of Salford there are no deacons. I think that it is necessary to be very careful in choosing the right men. Perhaps some parish priests have not really seen the possible roles in which permanent deacons can function and are therefore not in favour of them.

The ecumenical scene is a difficult one at present. It seems to me that we have to be realistic. The theological divides, which exist between us, have not been resolved and the recent difficulties in the Anglican Communion have not helped. Yet Christians working together can achieve much. The ecumenical Justice and Peace group in the parish did much in real terms. Fair trade work and the visits of the children from Chernobyl stand out.

Fr. Edmund had done much to help parishioners participate more fully in the running of the parish and I am sure that this will bear fruit. This is needed not just because of the shortage of priests. Catholicism is a social religion in which working for each other strengthens our bonds of faith. The number of people involved in various works was considerable. I cannot mention them all here but help was given in all areas from Liturgy to maintenance.

Whilst there are always issues and strains in any parish, Warwick Bridge was blessed with many people with a good spirit and sound views. Life in small parishes is problematical in our present situation with our great shortage of priests, but we should not be despondent. The acorns are there from which the future will grow and as this book shows we are the inheritors of a great heritage. It is our duty to nurture things for the future.

My time in Warwick Bridge was much shorter than I would have liked. It was a time when I learned much and which I much enjoyed".

TOWARDS THE FUTURE

In 2002 Abbot Timothy was obliged to move Fr. Cassian Dickie to Knaresborough. He told the parish that he was unable to supply a resident priest for the parish of Our Lady and St. Wilfrid. He asked the parish to review the situation together and come to a conclusion about the alternatives, the parish could be returned to the Bishop of Lancaster who might be able to supply a resident priest or they could remain part of the Ampleforth family, be responsible for the operations of the parish, and he would supply a priests at Weekends for as long as possible. The parish met and decided to remain with Ampleforth. Fr. Abbot then appointed a trio of priests living in the Monastery of St. Benedict at Bamber Bridge, Preston to look after the parish with Fr. Bonaventure Knollys being the Parish Priest. The other priests were Fr. David O'Brien and Fr. Stephen Wright. This programme worked well during 2002, but Fr. Bonaventure was recalled to the Abbey in September. Fr. Stephen took on the technical role of Parish Priest from then on. In the winter of 2003 Fr. David, who was over eighty, found the travelling too much so Fr. Stephen continued to be the weekend parish priest. In 2004 Abbot Timothy asked Fr Stephen to go to live at Our Lady and St Michael's, Workington and join the community there.

Liturgical Celebration In 2003 Fr Stephen and the parish council decided to change the Sunday Mass time at Warwick Bridge to 11 a.m. to allow him to spend more time with the St. Ninian's community after their 9 a.m. Mass. A Holy Hour was begun on Saturday mornings from 10.30 including morning prayer at the Church. Friday evening Mass and Monday morning Mass also incorporated Evening and Morning prayer as a normal part of the celebration.

The Church In 2006 the Bishops' Conference of England and Wales with English Heritage chose A.W. Pugin's Church of Our Lady and St Wilfrid's to be celebrated as one of the exceptional Catholic Churches in a major publication 'A Glimpse of Heaven'. In 2007 the wooden benches in the Nave were refurbished.

The Parish House The Parish Council decided to invite tenants to live in the Parish House with Fr Stephen occupying the guest's bed-sitting room for the weekends. Fr Edmund had altered the internal layout of the house for this arrangement.

Mission In 2007 Bishop Patrick O'Donoghue established an initiative to assess the preparedness for mission of each of the parishes and deaneries because the diocese faced a reduction in the number of priests. Abbot Cuthbert Madden (who had succeeded Abbot Timothy at Ampleforth) informed the parish that the Warwick Bridge parish should be considered a full member of the St. Herbert's Deanery in

Carlisle and be subject to the decisions of the Bishop. As a result of enquiries made about the preparedness for Mission of parishes in the Diocese, the following report was issued concerning the parish.

> The parish of Our Lady and Wilfrid, including St Ninian, has a reasonable combined Mass attendance and a low sacramental index.

> The Abbot of Ampleforth has requested that parishes of the Ampleforth Mission within Lancaster Diocese participate in the Fit for Mission review. The Diocese of Lancaster gratefully acknowledges the invaluable work and leadership of the Benedictines in North and West Cumbria.

> One of the strengths of Our Lady and St Wilfrid, including St Ninian, is the good level of lay leadership and participation in the sacramental and mission life. A particular strength is the commitment of the team of catechists. A further strength is the parish's successful vocations culture, particularly its programmes to discern and nominate candidates to the diaconate. This is commended to the diocese.

> Another strength is the parish's mission with families, through a range of activities that make up for the absence of a local school.

> Subject to the agreement of the Abbot of Ampleforth, the parish of Our Lady and St Wilfrid, Warwick Bridge, including St Ninian, Brampton, would continue under the care of Benedictine priests from Ampleforth Abbey for the foreseeable future.

At first sight this report may give the impression that Our Lady and St. Wilfrid is a thriving parish with the laity coping very well indeed with the problems caused by the fact that Warwick Bridge no longer has a resident parish priest. However, earlier in these pages it was suggested that since the sixties the parish seemed in some ways to be declining. Confirmation of such a decline is bluntly given in the figures produced for the Diocese of Lancaster in which it is stated that since the 70's the number of people attending Mass regularly has more than halved. It seems that Our Lady and St Wilfrid in this respect shows a similar reduction. On the other hand, the way in which the parish has responded to the difficulties caused by only having a priest available at the weekend, is encouraging. Otherwise it would be a tragedy if a community that coped with the difficulties that it faced in the persecution of the 16th century should begin to lose its inheritance in the 21st century by indifference or neglect. Perhaps in this instance pessimistic conclusions should be treated with caution as these latest accounts suggest that the laity of the parish are willing and anxious to play their part in a revival of its activities.

Appendix 1 - Our Lady and Saint Wilfrid

When describing the church of Our Lady and St Wilfrid, it is helpful that Pugin himself has left us an account of his ideas in the building of the chapel at Warwick Bridge. Phoebe Staunton (1971) gives us a summary:

> "Pugin mentioned and included a view of the little church of St Mary (the dedication is actually to Our Lady and St Wilfrid) at Warwick Bridge, Cumberland, which he had designed in 1840. He could, indeed, have written his whole essay about this church, for it had every feature he declared as essential. Fortunately the church remains almost exactly as Pugin left it; its decoration is intact and its setting has not changed in the years since it was built. Its altar is in the east, which Pugin said was the "antient position". It stands higher than the land about it but not aloof from it, another Pugin essential. The ground immediately surrounding the church is a graveyard. Pugin was unalterably opposed to commercial cemeteries and to the churches which excluded 'the very remembrance of death... lest the visitors to these places might be shocked at the sight of tombs'.
>
> The interior illustrates perfectly how Pugin fulfilled each of his requirements. A porch and a font are in the western end; the nave is filled with simple seats; the pulpit is next to the chancel arch and on the epistle side; and the open timber roof is painted. The chancel screen carries a rood with the Madonna and St John, and the Crucifix between them and the screen and the rood are touched with colour and gold. The chancel is beautifully and fully appointed with sedilia, sacrarium and an Easter sepulchre. The altar, raised above the floor of the chancel the height of a series of steps, is equipped with metal objects of Pugin's design. Two small coronas still hang on either side of it. The painting of the roof, the diapering of the walls, and the gilding of the reredos were carried out by the craftsman who was later to decorate St Giles', Cheadle."

Staunton's glowing description of Pugin's designs may seem comprehensive enough, but a shortened version of notes left by Fr Edmund Hatton should also be of assistance to the visitor.

The Interior of the Church of Our Lady and St Wilfrid

On the north and south walls of the nave there are several ornamental roundels in memory of families and other people who were benefactors to the church. For example the central roundel on the south side has "Pray for the soul of Isabella, daughter of Philip Milburn of the Howe in the parish of Hayton, yeoman, a benefactress to this church, she died on April 27th 1841 aged 45 years, may she rest in peace"

On the eastern most roundel on the north side, "Of your charity pray for the souls of Henry Howard of Corby Esquire who died March 1st 1842 aged 84 years and of Catherine Mary his wife, daughter of Sir Richard Neave of Dagenham Park, Essex, Bart, who died January 16th 1849 aged 78 years. Benefactress of this church. Have mercy O Lord we beseech thee on the souls of our servants and grant them eternal rest through the merits of Jesus Christ Our Lord and Saviour."

The windows of the church are utilized in similar fashion. The window between two eastern most roundels on the north wall has, 'We pray for the repose of the soul of Ursula Mary Levin who died

January 1960 descendant of Sir Thomas More. Daughter of Philip and Clare Howard of Corby, widow of Sir H Lawson Bart and wife of Lt Col H Levin."

Note - the Sanctuary ceiling is of the Lamb and Flag, the pulpit has paintings of Our Lady and St Wilfrid and in the centre St Paul preaching with the inscription, 'We preach Christ crucified'.

Inscription round the chancel arch, "In this we have known the charity of God because he has laid down his life for us" and "My soul doth magnify the Lord and my Spirit hath rejoiced in God my Saviour".

The sepulchre was emphatically a central part of the official liturgy of Holy Week, designed to give dramatic expression to the Christian teaching on the power of Christ's cross and passion, but also on the doctrine of the eucharist.

Every church was obliged to provide one for Holy Week and the Easter ceremonies. In most places it was a moveable wooden frame adorned with drapery and carved or painted panels. In many churches it was a permanent architectural and sculptured feature. This might take the form of a niche in the north wall of the chancel or a table tomb on the north side of the High Altar. Much money was spent on lavish decoration and adornment of the Easter sepulchre, often with images of sleeping soldiers, Christ rising, the three Marys, adoring angels, etc.

In churches where the Easter sepulchre was also the tomb of a benefactor, it expressed the hope that the benefactor would share in the Resurrection of Christ. Most of these devotions stopped with the Reformation.

Rood Screens

The purpose of the rood screen was first and foremost to proclaim the centrality of the atoning death of Jesus Christ. The beam on which the rood was supported often had lights on it and was sometimes called the candle beam.

It was at once a barrier and yet no barrier. It was a set of windows which made a frame for the liturgical drama taking place in the Sanctuary.

No Christian church was considered properly equipped without its great rood ... almost invariably accompanied by the figures of the blessed Virgin Mary, St. John the Apostle and Evangelist. The great rood was the most prominent object in the church and met the eye of everyone on entering

Finally, the east most roundel on the south side has this inscription: "Good Christian people pray for the soul of Francis Warwick of Warwick Hall Esq who died 14th July 1772 aged 75 years, of Ann his sister, who died December 9th 1774 aged 76 years and of Jane, his wife, who died October 23rd-1778 in the 73rd year of her age. For the love of God and their neighbour they founded and endowed this mission at Warwick Bridge. Merciful Jesus give them rest. Amen.

Appendix 2 - St Wilfrid's Junior and Infant School

St. Wilfrid's Junior and Infant School opened in 1932. From the beginning till its close in 1973 it only had three headmistresses:

1932-1934   Mrs. Mathieson
1934-1944   Mrs. Carroll (the mother of Mrs. Costello)
1944-1973   Mrs. Costello

In 1990 Father Vidal and Father D'Arcy left an appreciation of the outstanding work achieved by Mrs. Costello in her long service.

Father Francis Vidal:

'Terry succeeded her mother, Elizabeth Carroll, as the headmistress of St. Wilfrid's Junior and Infant School in 1944. She was later joined by her husband George and they both taught until the school was closed in the summer of 1973. The numbers had dwindled to 19 and Terry was due for retirement. The wonderful work done by Terry and George was rewarded in 1971 when Abbot Basil Hume presented them both with Bene Merenti medals. George died in 1973. Terry continued to give religious instruction to the Junior and Infant children who thenceforth attended state schools, both at Warwick Bridge and Brampton. She prepared them wonderfully well for their first confessions and Communion and also for the Sacrament of Confirmation. After she handed over these instructions to the Cravens in 1987 she was active in promoting the retreats at Ampleforth for our parishioners. She often attended the Holy Week ceremonies at the Abbey with her friend Rita Smart. On December 8th of last year on her way to Mass at Warwick Square she had a stroke. She has borne her infirmity with great fortitude and now leaves to be nearer to John and Dorothy'.

Father Sigebert D'Arcy:

'I would like to express my appreciation of Mrs. Terry Costello as a priest who worked in the parish for six years and also from my knowledge of her work as a member of the Lancaster Diocesan Schools Commission. To the best of my knowledge Mrs. Costello was headmistress and a teacher in the school for about thirty years. The school maintained a very high standard. Mrs. Costello served the children in the school and their parents with the utmost generosity. She was a first class Catholic teacher. When she retired she continued instructing the Catholic children in the two county primary schools. She has merited the deepest gratitude of the priests and people of the parish'.

That the parishioners of Our Lady and St. Wilfrid should have a school of their own was remarkable considering the smallness of the congregation. The enterprise was made possible by the generosity of Mrs. Liddell of Warwick Hall who provided land for the school, and Mr. Philip Howard of Corby Castle who provided a house. Unfortunately, over the years the needs and expenses of the school made it almost impossible for the parishioners to keep it going particularly since it never succeeded in obtaining Aided Status. It was quite an achievement that it was maintained for over forty years. Nevertheless it was disheartening for all concerned when it closed in 1973

Appendix 3 - Parish Priests of Our Lady and St Wilfrid

After the Reformation, Benedictine priests resided when possible, with families at Naworth Castle, Corby Castle and Warwick Hall. Detailed information about this period is difficult to obtain.

Fr. Thomas Warwick, professed in 1698 was stationed at Warwick Hall sometime before 1729

Fr Placid Howard at Corby Castle	1728
Fr Maurice Buckley	1729
Fr Thomas Welch	1753 – 1764

Fr. Phillip Jefferson for one year then Fr. Kaye

The Mission and Parish of Our Lady and St Wilfrid

Parish Priests

Fr Ambrose Kaye OSB	1767 - 1777
Fr Anselm Bolas OSB	1777 - 1797
Fr Bernard Ryding OSB	1797 - 1834
Fr Vincent Dale OSB	1834 - 1838
Fr Wilfrid Ryan OSB	1838 - 1877
Fr Stanislaus Giles OSB	1877 - 1893
Fr Wulstan Barnett OSB	1893 - 1918
Fr Sigebert Cody OSB	1918 - 1933
Fr Leo Hayes OSB	1933 - 1943
Fr Basil Mawson OSB	1943 – 1944
Fr Richard Wright OSB	1944 – 1952
Fr Bruno Dawson OSB	1952 - 1955
Fr Laurence Bevenot OSB	1955 - 1964
Fr Cyprian Thompson OSB	1964 - 1966
Fr Gerard Sitwell OSB	1966 - 1969
Fr Francis Vidal OSB	1969 - 1989
Fr Edmund Hatton OSB	1990 – 1999
Fr Cassian Dickie OSB	1999 – 2002
Fr Stephen Wright OSB	2002 –

Appendix 4 - Important Dates in the History of the Parish

16th Century
Wetheral Priory, along with the other religious houses, was suppressed. Britain was broken by the Reformation though some families managed to remain true to the Catholic faith.

17th and early 18th Centuries
Local Catholics were served by Benedictine priests who acted as chaplains at Warwick Hall and Corby Castle.

1774   Warwick Hall, having passed out of Catholic hands, a chapel and presbytery were built by Fr Ambrose Kaye.

1782   Additional land was bought costing £360. Some fifty years later more ground was purchased for future use.

1841   The present church, designed by A.W.N. Pugin, was opened in place of the 'old chapel' which was no longer suitable. The new church cost £2,586. This was done through the generosity of the Howards of Corby who bought the older building.

1850   The English Catholic Hierarchy was restored. Cumberland was placed in the Diocese of Hexham and Newcastle.

1918   About this date a small room over a blacksmith's shop in Brampton was rented for the purpose of Sunday Mass.

1921   Benedictine nuns, formerly at Fort Augustus in Inverness-shire, came to Holme Eden (built about 1840), which was bought for them by Charles Liddell of Warwick Hall.

1924   A new Diocese of Lancaster was created. This included Cumberland.

1931   St. Wilfrid's School was built.

1935   This year was the 12th centenary of the death of St. Bede and parishioners joined a pilgrimage to Jarrow.

1937   The old Workhouse at Brampton was reconditioned to accommodate Basque refugee children. Fr Antonio Renteria, from Bilbao, ministered to them until 1943, by which time they had all returned home.

1938   The sanctuary decorations in the church at Warwick Bridge were restored and improvements made to the chapel at Brampton.

1950   The centenary of the restoration of the English Hierarchy was celebrated.

1955   Ashmore, Craw Hall, Brampton was purchased for £5,500, mostly raised by parishioners. Part of the house was converted into a chapel (St. Ninian's), and the rest rented to a local family. The first Mass was said there by Thomas Bernard Pearson, Auxiliary Bishop of Lancaster, in June 1956.

1956   The construction of the Rocket Site at Spadeadam brought many additional Catholics, who were served by the Columban Fathers, recently expelled from China.

1958   Carlisle's Octocentenary celebrations included a Mass on Brunton Park attended by 700 people, including some from Warwick Bridge.

1968   Fr. Gerard Sitwell, the parish priest, preached in Holme Eden church during Church Unity Week. Later the Vicar of Holme Eden visited Warwick Bridge.

1970   The church belfry, found to be unsafe in 1968 and taken down, was restored.

1973   St. Wilfrid's School was closed.

1976   Bishop Pearson preached at a United Service in Brampton.

1980   The St Benedict Centenary was celebrated by Solemn High Mass in the church and a Buffet Lunch at Holme Eden Abbey.

1983   The Benedictine nuns at Holme Eden dispersed and the Abbey was closed. The house became a home for the elderly in the following year.

1991   150th Anniversary of the Church of Our Lady and St Wilfrid.

1995   Centenary of the chapel at Brampton.

Appendix 5 - Penal Laws and Relief Acts

1559   Act of Supremacy: Monarch supreme governor of Church Of England, clergy to take oath of supremacy on pain of deprivation.

1559   Act of Uniformity: imposed Book of Common Prayer, one shilling fine for failure to attend church on Sunday.

1563   Forbidden to defend papal supremacy on pain of Praemunire; (forfeiture of property).

1571   Treason to call monarch heretic or schismatic, treason to introduce papal bulls.

1581   Treason to convert or to be converted to Catholicism, fine of £20 per month for recusancy.

1585   Treason for Jesuits or seminary priests to enter the country.

1587   Suspected recusant who failed to appear for trial incurred guilt.

1593   Recusants restricted to within five miles of their homes.

1605   Convicted recusants to receive Anglican communion once per annum~ on pain of fine and eventual forfeiture of property.

1605   Recusants barred from office and professions.

1678   Recusants barred from parliament.

1692   Recusants incur double land tax.

1699   Recusants barred from purchasing or inheriting land.

1778   Relief Act: Catholics permitted to own land.

1791   Relief Act: Catholic clergy permitted to exercise ministry.

1829,   Emancipation Act: Catholics permitted to hold office and to sit in parliament.

Appendix 6

The Treasures and Property of the Parish

Over the years the parish has been given objects of special artistic or spiritual importance.

PETRONIA

The bones of St. Petronia were discovered in the catacomb of St. Priscilla in Rome in 1840. They were brought back to England by Lord Marmaduke Constable Maxwell for his chapel at Everingham. From there they were taken to Corby Castle, Carlisle and then passed on to Our Lady & St. Wilfrid's Church at Warwick Bridge.

THE CALDBECK MISSAL

Caldbeck is nearer Workington than Warwick Bridge. In 1506 one Robert Cooke gave it an enormous Missal (50cm high): but the arms on the chief image page, which are usually those of the original donor, are of Legard family of Ganton, Yorks (east of Ampleforth). The missal is of the Sarum use (an early English variant of the Roman Rite), but has a handwritten page added for St Kentigern, whose fame used to extend south from Glasgow into Cumbria. It is not known how it came to Warwick Bridge, but someone hid it when missals were being destroyed, and perhaps it came via the Howards. Like many missals in use at the Reformation it has the Pope rubbed out from the Canon of the Mass (and St Thomas Becket from the calendar).

Note from Ampleforth Archives

THE SIXTEENTH CENTURY VESTMENTS

Two vestments were given to the parish which had particular local significance. They came from Corby Castle and the orpheries which were 16C now sewn onto 19C velvet cloth, have been associated by tradition with Mary, Queen of Scots.

THE TWO IVORY CRUCIFIXES

Two ivory crucifixes of Spanish origin are part of the valuable items in the parish.

THE RELIC OF THE TRUE CROSS

This Relic is of unknown origin, but sealed and inscribed as a genuine relic.

THE PUGIN TABERNACLE.

This tabernacle is one of the most valuable Pugin objects. It is now used for the Altar of Repose on Maundy Thursday.

THE ORGAN

Although not original to the Church, the organ fits perfectly into the architecture and acoustic structure of the Pugin design. With only 6 stops it is simple, clear and functional for accompanying the congregation.

THE STABLES.

Fr. Edmund in 1995 sold the old teacher's bungalow in Warwick Bridge to turn the old Stable block, now garages, into a Parish room. He also completed repair work on the Church and the Parish House and planted new apple trees in the orchard.

THE NEW CEMETERY.

When the Corby estate was sold, Sir John Howard gave Fr. Edmund a section of a field adjoining the North parish boundary to be a new cemetery. Surrounded by a beech hedge it has been laid out with an avenue of shrubs for the procession to the area of the graves.

Bibliography

Allanson. - Biography of the English Benedictines, Ed Anselm Cramer, Ampleforth Abbey Trustees 1999

Bossy, J. - The English Catholic Community 1570-1850, London 1975

Bouch, CML. - Prelates and People of the Lake Counties - Titus Wilson, Kendal 1948

Bradley, M. - An Outline History of the Howard Family-Corby 1968

Caraman, P - St Philip Howard, Catholic Truth Society 1985

Elvins, M. - The Sussex Martyrs - Catholic Truth Society 1983

Foley, BC, - Some People of Penal Times - Cathedral Bookshop
        Ibid, - Some More People of Penal Times

Gwynn, D. - The Struggle for Catholic Emancipation 1750-1829 - London 1928

Hilton, J.A. - The Cumbrian Catholics - Northern History Vol XVI, Leeds University School of History

Hilton, J.A - The Recusant Historian's Handbook – North West Catholic History Society 1993

Hughes, P. - The Reformation in England: Religio Depopulata – Hollis and Carter 1954

Mullett and Warren - Martyrs of the Diocese of Lancaster - Rome 1987

Norman, E. - The English Catholic Church in the Nineteenth Century - OUP1984

The Duke of Norfolk. - The Lives of Philip Howard Earl of Arundel and Anne Dacres his Wife - Hurst and Blackett 1857

Orme, N (Ed.) - Nicholas Roscarrock's Lives of the Saints, Cornwall and Devon – Devon and Cornwall Record Society 1992.

Phythian-Adams, C. - Land of the Cumbrians, Scolar Press 1996

Reinmuth, HS - Lord William Howard and his Catholic Associations - 16th Conference on Post-Reformation Catholic History

Staunton, P. - Pugin. Thames and Hudson 1971

Spence, P. - St John Boste of Dufton - Appleby Business Services 1994

Surtees Society - Selections from the Household Books of Lord William Howard - Ed, G. Ormsby 1877

Vaughan, F.J. – Border Catholics in 1687 – Cumbria Family History Society. May 1983